ECHOES

FROM THE SOUTH.

COMPRISING

THE MOST IMPORTANT SPEECHES, PROCLAMATIONS, AND PUBLIC ACTS EMANATING FROM THE SOUTH DURING THE LATE WAR.

NEW YORK:
E. B. TREAT & CO.

BALTIMORE, Md., L. T. PALMER & CO. ST. LOUIS, Mo., I. S. BRAINARD.
LOUISVILLE, Ky., G. B. FESSENDEN & CO.
CHARLESTON, S. C., ROBT. WILSON. MEMPHIS, Tenn., J. B. SUTTON.
GEO. W. LOYD, AUGUSTA, Ga., and AUBURN, Ala.

MACDONALD & STONE, PRINTERS AND STEREOTYPERS, 49 CENTRE STREET, N. Y

NOTICE.

The Publishers present this little volume to the public in the belief that a record of the great speeches and public acts emanating from the South during the late struggle, will prove, as a matter of History, both valuable and interesting to all classes of readers.

CONTENTS.

ECHOES FROM THE SOUTH.

SPEECH OF HON. A. H. STEPHENS,

DELIVERED IN THE HALL OF THE HOUSE OF REPRESENTATIVES OF GEORGIA, NOV. 14, 1860.

FELLOW-CITIZENS: I appear before you to-night at the request of members of the Legislature and others to speak of matters of the deepest interest that can possibly concern us all of an earthly character. There is nothing—no question or subject connected with this life—that concerns a free people so intimately as that of the Government under which they live. We are now, indeed, surrounded by evils. Never since I entered upon the public stage has the country been so environed with difficulties and dangers that threatened the public peace and the very existence of society as now. I do not now appear before you at my own instance. It is not to gratify desire of my own that I am here. Had I consulted my own ease and pleasure I should not be before you; but, believing that it is the duty of every good citizen to give his counsels and views whenever the country is in danger, as to the best policy to be pursued, I am here. For these reasons, and these only, do I bespeak a calm, patient, and attentive hearing.

My object is not to stir up strife, but to allay it; not to appeal to your passions, but to your reason. Good governments can never be built up or sustained by the impulse of passion. I wish to address myself to your good sense, to your good judgment, and if after hearing you disagree, let us agree to disagree, and part as we met, friends. We all have the same object, the same interest. That people should disagree in republican governments, upon questions of public policy, is natural. That men should disagree upon all matters connected with human investigation, whether relating to science or human conduct, is natural. Hence, in free governments, parties will arise. But a free people should express their different opinions with liberality and charity, with no acrimony towards those of their fellows, when honestly and sincerely given. These are my feelings to-night.

Let us, therefore, reason together. It is not my purpose to say aught to wound the feelings of any individual who may be present; and if in the ardency with which I shall express my opinions, I shall say anything which may be deemed too strong, let it be set down to the zeal with which I advocate my own convictions. There is with me no intention to irritate or offend.

The first question that presents itself is, shall the people of the South secede from the Union in consequence of the election of Mr. Lincoln to the presidency of the United States? My countrymen, *I tell you frankly, candidly, and earnestly, that I do not think that they ought.* In my judgment, the election of no man, constitutionally chosen to that high office, is sufficient cause for any State to separate from the Union. It ought to stand by and aid still in maintaining the constitution of the country. To make a point of resistance to the Government, to withdraw from it because a man has been constitutionally elected, puts us in the wrong. We are pledged to maintain the Constitution. Many of us have sworn to support it. Can we, therefore, for the mere election of a man to the Presidency, and that, too, in accordance with the prescribed forms of the Constitution, make a point of resistance to the Government without becoming the breakers of that sacred instrument ourselves, withdraw ourselves from it? Would we not be in the wrong? Whatever fate is to befall this country, let it never be laid to the charge of the people of the South, and especially to the people of Georgia, that we were untrue to our national engagements. Let the fault and the wrong rest upon others. If all our hopes are to be blasted, if the Republic is to go down, let us be found to the last moment standing on the deck, with the Constitution of the United States waving over our heads. (Applause.) Let the fanatics of the North break the Constitution, if such is their fell purpose. Let the responsibility be upon them. I shall speak presently more of their acts; but let not the South, let us not be the ones to commit the aggression. We went into the election with this people. The result was different from what we wished; but the election has been constitutionally held. Were we to make a point of resistance to the Government and go out of the Union on that account, the record would be made up hereafter against us.

But it is said Mr. Lincoln's policy and principles are against the Constitution, and that if he carries them out it will be destructive of our rights. Let us not anticipate a threatened evil. If he violates the Constitution then will come our time to act. Do not let us break it because, forsooth, he may. If he does, that is the time for us to strike. (Applause.) I think it would be injudicious and unwise to do this sooner. I do not anticipate that Mr. Lincoln will do anything to jeopardize our safety or security, whatever may be his spirit to do it; for he is bound by the constitutional checks which are thrown around him, which at this time renders him powerless to do any great mischief. This shows the wisdom of our system. The President of the United States is no emperor, no dictator—he is clothed with no absolute power. He can do nothing unless he is backed by power in Congress. The House of Representatives is largely in the majority against him.

In the Senate he will also be powerless. There will be a majority of four against him. This, after the loss of Bigler, Fitch, and others, by the unfortunate dissensions of the National Democratic party in their States. Mr. Lincoln cannot appoint an officer without the consent of the Senate—he cannot form a Cabinet without the same consent. He will be in the condition of George III., (the embodiment of Toryism,) who had to ask the Whigs to appoint his ministers, and was compelled to receive a cabinet utterly opposed to his views; and so Mr. Lincoln will be compelled to ask of the Senate to choose for him a cabinet, if the Democracy of that body choose to put him on such terms. He will be compelled to do this or let the Government stop, if the National Democratic men—for that is their name at the North—the conservative men in the Senate, should so determine. Then, how can Mr. Lincoln obtain a cabinet which would aid him, or allow him to violate the Constitution?

Why then, I say, should we disrupt the ties of this Union when his hands are tied, when he can do nothing against us? I have heard it mooted that no man in the State of Georgia, who is true to her interests, could hold office under Mr. Lincoln. But, I ask, who appoints to office? Not the President alone; the Senate has to concur. No man can be appointed without the consent of the Senate. Should any man then refuse to hold office that was given to him by a Democratic Senate? [Mr. Toombs interrupted and said if the Senate was Democratic it was for Mr. Breckinridge.] Well, then, continued Mr. S., I apprehend no man could be justly considered untrue to the interests of Georgia, or incur any disgrace, if the interests of Georgia required it, to hold an office which a Breckinridge Senate had given him, even though Mr. Lincoln should be President. (Prolonged applause, mingled with interruptions.)

I trust, my countrymen, you will be still and

silent. I am addressing your good sense. I am giving you my views in a calm and dispassionate manner, and if any of you differ with me, you can, on any other occasion, give your views as I am doing now, and let reason and true patriotism decide between us. In my judgment, I say, under such circumstances, there would be no possible disgrace for a Southern man to hold office. No man will be suffered to be appointed, I have no doubt, who is not true to the Constitution, if Southern Senators are true to their trusts, as I cannot permit myself to doubt that they will be.

My honorable friend who addressed you last night, (Mr. Toombs,) and to whom I listened with the profoundest attention, asks if we would submit to Black Republican rule? I say to you and to him, as a Georgian, I never would submit to any Black Republican *aggression* upon our constitutional rights. I will never consent myself, as much as I admire this Union for the glories of the past, or the blessings of the present, as much as it has done for the people of all these States, as much as it has done for civilization, as much as the hopes of the world hang upon it, I would never submit to aggression upon my rights to maintain it longer; and if they cannot be maintained in the Union, standing on the Georgia platform, where I have stood from the time of its adoption, I would be in favor of disrupting every tie which binds the States together.

I will have equality for Georgia and for the citizens of Georgia in this Union, or I will look for new safeguards elsewhere. This is my position. The only question now is, can they be secured in the Union? That is what I am counselling with you to-night about. Can it be secured? In my judgment it may be, but it may not be; but let us do all we can, so that in the future, if the worst come, it may never be said we were negligent in doing our duty to the last.

My countrymen, I am not of those who believe this Union has been a curse up to this time. True men, men of integrity, entertain different views from me on this subject. I do not question their right to do so; I would not impugn their motives in so doing. Nor will I undertake to say that this Government of our fathers is perfect. There is nothing perfect in this world of a human origin. Nothing connected with human nature, from man himself to any of his works. You may select the wisest and best men for your judges, and yet how many defects are there in the administration of justice? You may select the wisest and best men for your legislators, and yet how many defects are apparent in your laws? And it is so in our Government.

But that this Government of our fathers, with all its defects, comes nearer the objects of all good Governments than any other on the face of the earth is my settled conviction. Contrast it now with any on the face of the earth. [England, said Mr. Toombs.]—England, my friend says. Well, that is the next best, I grant; but I think we have improved upon England. Statesmen tried their apprentice hand on the Government of England, and then ours was made. Ours sprung from that, avoiding many of its defects, taking most of the good and leaving out many of its errors, and from the whole constructing and building up this model Republic—the best which the history of the world gives an account of.

Compare, my friends, this Government with that of Spain, Mexico, and South American Republics, Germany, Ireland—are there any sons of that downtrodden nation here to-night?—Prussia, or if you travel further East, to Turkey or China. Where will you go, following the sun in its circuit round our globe, to find a Government that better protects the liberties of its people, and secures to them the blessings we enjoy? (Applause.) I think that one of the evils that beset us is a surfeit of liberty, an exuberance of the priceless blessings for which we are ungrateful. We listened to my honorable friend who addressed you last night, (Mr. Toombs,) as he recounted the evils of this Government.

The first was the fishing bounties, paid mostly to the sailors of New England. Our friend stated that forty-eight years of our Government was under the administration of Southern Presidents. Well, these fishing bounties began under the rule of a Southern President, I believe. No one of them during the whole forty-eight years ever set his Administration against the principle or policy of them. It is not for me to say whether it was a wise policy in the beginning; it probably was not, and I have nothing to say in its defence. But the reason given for it was to encourage our young men to go to sea and learn to manage ships. We had at the time but a small navy. It was thought best to encourage a class of our people to become acquainted with seafaring life; to become sailors; to man our naval ships. It requires practice to walk the deck of a ship, to pull the ropes, to furl the sails, to go aloft, to climb the mast; and it was thought, by offering this bounty, a nursery might be formed in which young men would become perfected in these arts, and it applied to one section of the country as well as to any other.

The result of this was, that in the war of 1812 our sailors, many of whom came from this nursery, were equal to any that England brought against us. At any rate, no small part of the glories of that war were gained by the veteran tars of America, and the object of these bounties was to foster that branch of the national defence. My opinion is, that whatever may have been the reason at first, this bounty ought to be discontinued—the reason for it at first no longer exists. A bill for this object did pass the Senate the last Congress I was in, to which my honorable friend contributed greatly, but it was not reached in the House of Representatives. I trust that he will yet see that he may with honor continue his connection with the Government, and that his eloquence, unrivalled in the Senate, may hereafter, as heretofore, be displayed in having this bounty, so obnoxious to him, repealed and wiped off from the statute book.

The next evil that my friend complained of was the Tariff. Well, let us look at that for a moment. About the time I commenced noticing public matters, this question was agitating the country almost as fearfully as the slave question now is. In 1832, when I was in college, South Carolina was ready to nullify or secede from the Union on this account. And what have we seen? The Tariff no longer distracts the public councils. Reason has triumphed! The present Tariff was voted for by

Massachusetts and South Carolina. The lion and the lamb lay down together—every man in the Senate and House from Massachusetts and South Carolina, I think, voted for it, as did my honorable friend himself. And if it be true, to use the figure of speech of my honorable friend, that every man in the North that works in iron and brass and wood has his muscle strengthened by the protection of the Government, that stimulant was given by his vote, and I believe every other Southern man. So we ought not to complain of that.

Mr. Toombs—The tariff assessed the duties.

Mr. Stephens—Yes, and Massachusetts with unanimity voted with the South to lessen them, and they were made just as low as Southern men asked them to be, and that is the rates they are now at. If reason and argument, with experience, produced such changes in the sentiments of Massachusetts from 1832 to 1857, on the subject of the Tariff, may not like changes be effected there by the same means—reason and argument, and appeals to patriotism on the present vexed question; and who can say that by 1875 or 1890 Massachusetts may not vote with South Carolina and Georgia upon all those questions that now distract the country, and threaten its peace and existence. I believe in the power and efficiency of truth, in the omnipotence of truth, and its ultimate triumph when properly wielded. (Applause.)

Another matter of grievance alluded to by my honorable friend was the navigation laws. This policy was also commenced under the Administration of one of these Southern Presidents who ruled so well, and has been continued through all of them since. The gentleman's views of the policy of these laws and my own do not disagree. We occupied the same ground in relation to them in Congress. It is not my purpose to defend them now. But it is proper to state some matters connected with their origin.

One of the objects was to build up a commercial American marine by giving American bottoms the exclusive carrying trade between our own ports. This is a great arm of national power. This object was accomplished. We have now an amount of shipping, not only coastwise, but to foreign countries, which puts us in the front rank of the nations of the world. England can no longer be styled the Mistress of the Seas. What American is not proud of the result? Whether those laws should be continued is another question. But one thing is certain: no President, Northern or Southern, has ever yet recommended their repeal. And my friend's efforts to get them repealed were met with but little favor, North or South.

These, then, were the true main grievances or grounds of complaint against the general system of our Government and its workings—I mean the administration of the Federal Government. As to the acts of the Federal States, I shall speak presently, but these three were the main ones used against the common head. Now, suppose it be admitted that all of these are evils in the system, do they overbalance and outweigh the advantages and great good which this same Government affords in a thousand innumerable ways that cannot be estimated? Have we not at the South, as well as at the North, grown great, prosperous, and happy under its operation? Has any part of the world ever shown such rapid progress in the development of wealth, and all the material resources of national power and greatness, as the Southern States have under the General Government, notwitstanding all its defects?

Mr. TOOMBS—In spite of it.

Mr. STEPHENS—My honorable friends says we have, in spite of the General Government; that without it I suppose he thinks we might have done as well, or perhaps, than we have done this in spite of it. That may be, and it may not be; but the great fact that we have grown great and powerful under the Government as it exists, there is no conjecture or speculation about that; it stands out bold, high, and prominent like your Stone Mountain, to which the gentleman alluded in illustrating home facts in his record—this great fact of our unrivalled prosperity in the Union as it is admitted; whether all this in spite of the Government—whether we of the South would have been better off without the Government—is, to say the least, problematical. On the one side we can only put the fact against speculation and conjecture on the other. But even as a question of speculation I differ with my distinguished friend.

What we would have lost in border wars without the Union, or what we have gained simply by the peace it has secured, no estimate can be made of. Our foreign trade, which is the foundation of all our prosperity, has the protection of the navy, which drove the pirates from the waters near our coast, where they had been buccaneering for centuries before, and might have been still had it not been for the American Navy under the command of such spirits as Commodore Porter. Now that the coast is clear, that our commerce flows freely outwardly, we cannot well estimate how it would have been under other circumstances. The influence of the

Government on us is like that of the atmosphere around us. Its benefits are so silent and unseen that they are seldom thought of or appreciated.

We seldom think of the single element of oxygen in the air we breathe, and yet let this simple, unseen, and unfelt agent be withdrawn, this life-giving element be taken away from this all-pervading fluid around us, and what instant and appalling changes would take place in all organic creation.

It may be that we are all that we are in "spite of the General Government," but it may be that without it we should have been far different from what we are now. It is true there is no equal part of the earth with natural resources superior perhaps to ours. That portion of this country known as the Southern States, stretching from the Chesapeake to the Rio Grande, is fully equal to the picture drawn by the honorable and eloquent Senator last night, in all natural capacities. But how many ages and centuries passed before these capacities were developed to reach this advanced age of civilization? There these same hills, rich in ore, same rivers, same valleys and plains, are as they have been since they came from the hand of the Creator; uneducated and uncivilized man roamed over them for how long no history informs us.

It was only under our institutions that they could

be developed. Their development is the result of the enterprise of our people under operations of the Government and institutions under which we have lived. Even our people without these never would have done it. The organization of society has much to do with the development of the natural resources of any country or any land. The institutions of a people, political and moral, are the matrix in which the germ of their organic structure quickens into life takes root and develops in form, nature and character. Our institutions constitute the basis, the matrix, from which spring all our characteristics of development and greatness. Look at Greece. There is the same fertile soil, the same blue sky, the same inlets and harbors, the same Ægean, the same Olympus; there is the same land where Homer sung, where Pericles spoke; it is in nature the same old Greece—but it is living Greece no more. (Applause.)

Descendants of the same people inhabit the country; yet what is the reason of this mighty difference? In the midst of present degradation we see the glorious fragments of ancient works of art—temples with ornaments and inscriptions that excite wonder and admiration—the remains of a once high order of civilization which have outlived the language they spoke—upon them all Ichabod is written—their glory has departed. Why is this so? I answer, their institutions have been destroyed. These were but the fruits of their forms of goverment, the matrix from which their grand development sprung, and when once the institutions of a people have been destroyed, there is no earthly power that can bring back the Promethean spark to kindle them here again, any more than in that ancient land of eloquence, poetry, and song. (Applause.)

The same may be said of Italy. Where is Rome, once the mistress of the world? There are the same seven hills now, the same soil, the same natural resources; nature is the same, but what a ruin of human greatness meets the eye of the traveller throughout the length and breadth of that most downtrodden land! Why have not the people of that Heaven-favored clime the spirit that animated their fathers? Why this sad difference?

It is the destruction of her institutions that has caused it; and, my countrymen, if we shall in an evil hour rashly pull down and destroy those institutions which the patriotic band of our fathers labored so long and so hard to build up, and which have done so much for us and the world, who can venture the prediction that similar results will not ensue? Let us avoid it if we can. I trust the spirit is among us that will enable us to do it. Let us not rashly try the experiment, for if it fails as it did in Greece and

Italy, and in the South American Republics, and in every other place, wherever liberty is once destroyed, it may never be restored to us again. (Applause.)

There are defects in our Government, errors in administration, and shortcomings of many kinds, but in spite of these defects and errors, Georgia has grown to be a great State. Let us pause here a moment. In 1850 there was a great crisis, but not so fearful as this, for of all I ever passed through, this is the most perilous, and requires to be met with the greatest calmness and deliberation.

There were many amongst us in 1850 zealous to go at once out of the Union, to disrupt every tie that binds us together. Now do you believe, had that policy been carried out at that time, we would have been the same great people that we are to-day? It may be that we would, but have you any assurance of that fact? Would you have made the same advancement, improvement, and progress in all that constitutes material wealth and prosperity that we have?

I notice in the Comptroller-General's report, that the taxable property of Georgia is $670,000,000 and upwards, an amount not far from double that it was in 1850. I think I may venture to say that for the last ten years the material wealth of the people of Georgia has been nearly if not quite doubled. The same may be said of our advance in education, and every thing that marks our civilization. Have we any assurance that had we regarded the earnest but misguided patriotic advice, as I think, of some of that day, and disrupted the ties which bind us to the Union, we would have advanced as we have? I think not. Well, then, let us be careful now before we attempt any rash experiment of this sort. I know that there are friends whose patriotism I do not intend to question, who think this Union a curse, and that we would be better off without it. I do not so think; if we can bring about a correction of these evils which threaten—and I am not without hope that this may not yet be done—this appeal to go out, with all the provisions for good that accompany it, I look upon as a great and I fear a fatal temptation.

When I look around and see our prosperity in every thing, agriculture, commerce, art, science, and every department of education, physical and mental, as well as moral advancement, and our colleges, I think, in the face of such an exhibition, if we can without the loss of power, or any essential right or interest, remain in the Union, it is our duty to ourselves and to posterity to—let us not too readily yield to this temptation—do so. Our first parents, the great progenitors of the human race, were not without a like temptation when in the Garden of

Eden. They were led to believe that their condition would be bettered—that their eyes would be opened—and that they would become as gods. They in an evil hour yielded—instead of becoming gods they only saw their own nakedness.

I look upon this country with our institutions as the Eden of the world, the paradise of the universe. It may be that out of it we may become greater and more prosperous, but I am candid and sincere in telling you that I fear if we rashly evince passion and without sufficient cause shall take that step, that instead of becoming greater or more peaceful, prosperous, and happy—instead of becoming gods, we will become demons, and at no distant day commence cutting one another's throats. This is my apprehension. Let us, therefore, whatever we do, meet these difficulties, great as they are, like wise and sensible men, and consider them in the light of all the consequences which may attend our action. Let us see first clearly where the path of duty leads, and then we may not fear to tread therein.

I come now to the main question put to me, and on which my counsel has been asked. That is, what the present Legislature should do in view of the dangers that threaten us, and the wrongs that have been done us by several of our Confederate States in the Union, by the acts of their legislatures nullifying the fugitive slave law, and in direct disregard of their constitutional obligations. What I shall say will not be in the spirit of dictation. It will be simply my own judgment for what it is worth. It proceeds from a strong conviction that according to it our rights, interests, and honor—our present safety and future security can be maintained without yet looking to the last resort, the "*ultima ratio regum.*" That should not be looked to until all else fails. That may come. On this point I am hopeful, but not sanguine. But let us use every patriotic effort to prevent it while there is ground for hope.

If any view that I may present, in your judgment, be inconsistent with the best interests of Georgia, I ask you, as patriots, not to regard it. After hearing me and others whom you have advised with, act in the premises according to your own conviction of duty as patriots. I speak now particularly to the members of the Legislature present. There are, as I have said, great dangers ahead. Great dangers may come from the election I have spoken of. If the policy of Mr. Lincoln and his Republican associates shall be carried out, or attempted to be carried out, no man in Georgia will be more willing or ready than myself to defend our rights, interest, and honor at every hazard, and to the last extremity. (Applause.)

What is this policy? It is in the first place to exclude us by an act of Congress from the Territories with our slave property. He is for using the power of the General Government against the extension of our institutions. Our position on this point is and ought to be, at all hazards, for perfect equality between all the States, and the citizens of all the States, in the Territories, under the Constitution of the United States. If Congress should exercise its power against this, then I am for standing where Georgia planted herself in 1850. These were plain propositions which were then laid down in her celebrated platform as sufficient for the disruption of the Union if the occasion should ever come; on these Georgia has declared that she will go out of the Union; and for these she would be justified by the nations of the earth in so doing.

I say the same; I said it then; I say it now, if Mr. Lincoln's policy should be carried out. I have told you that I do not think his bare election sufficient cause: but if his policy should be carried out in violation of any of the principles set forth in the Georgia Platform, that would be such an act of aggression which ought to be met as therein provided for. If his policy shall be carried out in repealing or modifying the Fugitive Slave law so as to weaken its efficacy, Georgia has declared that she will in the last resort disrupt the ties of the Union, and I say so too. I stand upon the Georgia Platform, and upon every plank, and say if those aggressions therein provided for take place, I say to you and the people of Georgia, keep your powder dry, and let your assailants then have lead, if need be. (Applause.) I would wait for an act of aggression. This is my position.

Now, upon another point, and that the most difficult and deserving your most serious consideration, I will speak. That is the course which this State should pursue towards these Northern States, which by their legislative acts have attempted to nullify the Fugitive Slave law. I know that in some of these States their acts pretend to be based upon the principles set forth in the case of Prigg against Pennsylvania; that decision did proclaim the doctrine that the State officers are not bound to carry out the provisions of a law of Congress—that the Federal Government cannot impose duties upon State officials; that they must execute their own laws by their own officers. And this may be true. But still it is the duty of the States to deliver fugitive slaves, as well as the duty of the General Government to see that it is done.

Northern States, on entering into the Federal compact, pledged themselves to surrender such fugitives; and it is in disregard of their obligations that they have passed laws which even tend to hinder or obstruct the fulfilment of that obligation. They have violated their plighted faith; what ought we to do in view of this? That is the question. What is to be done? By the law of nations you would have a right to demand the carrying out of this article of agreement, and I do not see that it should be otherwise with respect to the States of this Union; and in case it be not done, we would, by these principles, have the right to commit acts of reprisal on these faithless Governments, and seize upon their property, or that of their citizens, where-ever found. The States of this Union stand upon the same footing with foreign nations in this respect. But by the law of nations we are equally bound, before proceeding to violent measures, to set forth our grievances before the offending Government, to give them an opportunity to redress the wrong. Has our State yet done this? I think not.

Suppose it were Great Britain that had violated some compact of agreement with the General Government, what would be first done? In that case our Minister would be directed in the first instance to bring the matter to the attention of that Government, or a Commissioner be sent to that country to open negotiations with her, ask for redress, and it would only be when argument and reason had been exhausted that we should take the last resort of nations. That would be the course towards a foreign Government, and towards a member of this Confederacy I would recommend the same course.

Let us, therefore, not act hastily in this matter. Let your Committee on the State of the Republic make out a bill of grievances; let it be sent by the Governor to those faithless States, and if reason and argument shall be tried in vain—all shall fail to induce them to return to their constitutional obligations, I would be for retaliatory measures, such as the Governor has suggested to you. This mode of resistance to the Union is in our power. It might be effectual, and if in the last resort, we would be justified in the eyes of nations, not only in separating from them, but by using force.

[Some one said the argument was already exhausted.]

Mr. Stephens continued—Some friend says that the argument is already exhausted. No, my friend, it is not. You have never called the attention of the Legislatures of those States to this subject, that I am aware of. Nothing has ever been done before this year. The attention of our own people has been called to this subject lately.

Now, then, my recommendation to you would be this: In view of all these questions of difficulty, let a convention of the people of Georgia be called, to which they may be all referred. Let the sovereignty of the people speak. Some think that the election of Mr. Lincoln is cause sufficient to dissolve the Union. Some think those other grievances are sufficient to dissolve the same, and that the Legislature has the power thus to act, and ought thus to act. I have no hesitancy in saying that the Legislature is not the proper body to sever our Federal relations, if that necessity should arise. An honorable and distinguished gentleman, the other night, (Mr. T. R. R. Cobb,) advised you to take this course—not to wait to hear from the cross-roads and groceries. I say to you, you have no power so to act. You must refer this question to the people and you must wait to hear from the men at the cross-roads and even the groceries; for the people in this country, whether at the cross-roads or the groceries, whether in cottages or palaces, are all equal, and they are the sovereigns in this country. Sovereignty is not in the Legislature. We, the people, are the sovereigns. I am one of them and have a right to be heard, and so has any other citizen of the State. You legislators, I speak it respectfully, are but our servants. You are the servants of the people, and not their masters. Power resides with the people in this country.

The great difference between our country and all others, such as France and England and Ireland, is, that here there is popular sovereignty, while there sovereignty is exercised by kings and favored classes. This principle of popular sovereignty, however much derided lately, is the foundation of our institutions. Constitutions are but the channels through which the popular will may be expressed. Our Constitution came from the people. They made it, and they alone can rightfully unmake it.

Mr. TOOMBS— I am afraid of conventions.

Mr. STEPHENS—I am not afraid of any convention legally chosen by the people. I know no way to decide great questions affecting fundamental laws except by representatives of the people. The Constitution of the United States was made by the representatives of the people. The Constitution of the State of Georgia was made by representatives of the people chosen at the ballot-box. But do not let the question which comes before the people be put to them in the language of my honorable friend who addressed you last night. Will you submit to abolition rule or resist?

Mr. TOOMBS—I do not wish the people to be cheated.

Mr. STEPHENS—Now, my friends, how are we going to cheat the people by calling on them to elect delegates to a convention to decide all these questions without any dictation or direction? Who proposes to cheat the people by letting them speak their own untrammelled views in the choice of their ablest and best men, to determine upon all these matters, involving their peace.

I think the proposition of my honorable friend had a considerable smack of unfairness, not to say cheat. He wished to have no convention, but for the Legislature to submit their vote to the people—submission to abolition rule or resistance? Now, who in Georgia would vote "submission to abolition rule?" (Laughter.)

Is putting such a question to the people to vote on, a fair way of getting an expression of the popular will on all these questions? I think not. Now, who in Georgia is going to submit to abolition rule?

Mr. TOOMBS—The convention will.

Mr. STEPHENS—No, my friend, Georgia will never do it. The convention will never secede from the Georgia Platform. Under that there can be no abolition rule under the General Government. I am not afraid to trust the people in convention upon this and all questions. Besides, the Legislature were not elected for such a purpose. They came here to do their duty as legislators. They have sworn to support the Constitution of the United States. They did not come here to disrupt this Government. I am, therefore, for submitting all these questions to a convention of the people. Submit this question to the people, whether they would submit to abolition rule or resist, and then let the Legislature act upon that vote! Such a course would be an insult to the people. They would have to eat their platform, ignore their past history, blot out their records, and take steps backwards, if they should do this. I have never eaten my record or words, and never will.

But how will it be under this arrangement if they should vote to resist, and the Legislature should re-assemble with this vote as their instruction? Can any man tell me what sort of resistance will be meant? One man would say secede; another pass retaliatory measures; these are measures of resistance against wrong—legitimate and right—and there would be as many different ideas as there are members on this floor. Resistance don't mean secession—that in no proper sense of the term is resistance. Believing that the times require action, I am for presenting the question fairly to the people, for calling together an untrammelled convention, and presenting all the questions to them whether they will go out of the Union, or what course of resistance in the

Union they may think best, and then let the Legislature act, when the people in their majesty are heard, and I tell you now, whatever that convention does, I hope and trust our people will abide by. I advise the calling of a convention with the earnest desire to preserve the peace and harmony of the State. I should dislike above all things to see violent measures adopted, or a disposition to take the sword in hand, by individuals, without the authority of law.

My honorable friend said last night, " I ask you to give me the sword, for if you do not give it to me, as God lives, I will take it myself."

Mr. Toombs—I will. (Applause on the other side.)

Mr. Stephens—I have no doubt that my honorable friend feels as he says. It is only his excessive ardor that makes him use such an expression; but this will pass off with the excitement of the hour. When the people in their majesty shall speak, I have no doubt that he will bow to their will, whatever it may be, upon the "sober second thought." (Applause.)

Should Georgia determine to go out of the Union, I speak for one, though my views might not agree with them, whatever the result may be, I shall bow to the will of her people. Their cause is my cause, and their destiny is my destiny; and I trust this will be the ultimate course of all. The greatest curse that can befall a free people is civil war.

But, as I said, let us call a convention of the people; let all these matters be submitted to it, and when the will of the majority of the people has thus been expressed, the whole State will present one unanimous voice in favor of whatever may be demanded; for I believe in the power of the people to govern themselves when wisdom prevails and passion is silent.

Look at what has already been done by them for their advancement in all that ennobles man. There is nothing like it in the history of the world. Look abroad, from one extent of the country to the other, contemplate our greatness. We are now among the first nations of the earth. Shall it be said, then, that our institutions, founded upon principles of self-government, are a failure?

Thus far it is a noble example, worthy of imitation. The gentleman, Mr. Cobb, the other night said it had proven a failure. A failure in what? In growth? Look at our expanse in national power. Look at our population and increase in all that makes a people great. A failure? Why are we the admiration of the civilized world, and present the brightest hopes of mankind.

Some of our public men have failed in their aspirations; that is true, and from that comes a great part of our troubles. (Prolonged applause.)

No, there is no failure of this Government yet. We have made great advancement under the Constitution, and I cannot but hope that we shall advance higher yet. Let us be true to our cause.

Now, when this convention assembles, if it shall be called, as I hope it may, I would say in my judgment, without dictation, for I am conferring with you freely and frankly, and it is thus that I give my views, I should take into consideration all those questions which distract the public mind; should view all the grounds of secession so far as the election of Mr. Lincoln is concerned, and I have no doubt they would say that the constitutional election of no man is a sufficient cause to break up the Union, but that the State should wait until he at least does some unconstitutional act.

Mr. TOOMBS—Commit some overt act.

Mr. STEPHENS—No, I did not say that. The word overt is a sort of technical term connected with treason, which has come to us from the mother country, and it means an open act of rebellion. I do not see how Mr. Lincoln can do this unless he should levy war upon us. I do not, therefore, use the word overt. I do not intend to wait for that. But I use the word unconstitutional act, which our people understand much better, and which expresses just what I mean. But as long as he conforms to the Constitution he should be left to exercise the duties of his office.

In giving this advice I am but sustaining the Constitution of my country, and I do not thereby become a Lincoln aid man either, (applause,) but a Constitutional aid man. But this matter the convention can determine.

As to the other matter, I think we have a right to pass retaliatory measures, provided they be in accordance with the Constitution of the United States, and I think they can be made such. But whether it would be wise for this Legislature to do this now is the question. To the convention, in my judgment, this matter ought to be referred. Before we commit reprisals on New England we should exhaust every means of bringing about a peaceful solution of the question.

Thus did Gen. Jackson in the case of the French. He did not recommend reprisals until he had treated with France, and got her to promise to make indemnification, and it was only on her refusal to pay the money which she had promised, that he recommended reprisals. It was after negotiation had failed. I do think, therefore, that it would be best, before going to extreme measures with our confederate States, to make presentation of our demands, to appeal to their reason and judgment to give us our rights. Then, if reason should not triumph, it will be time enough to commit reprisals, and we should be justified in the eyes of a civilized world. At least let the States know what your grievances are, and if they refuse, as I said, to give us our rights under the Constitution of our country, I should be willing, as a last resort, to sever the ties of this Union. (Applause.)

My own opinion is, that if this course be pursued, and they are informed of the consequences of refusal, these States will secede; but if they should not, then let the consequences be with them, and let the responsibility of the consequences rest upon them. Another thing I would have that convention to do. Reaffirm the Georgia Platform with an additional plank in it. Let that plank be the fulfilment of the obligation on the part of those States to repeal these obnoxious laws as a condition of our remaining in the Union. Give them time to consider it, and I would ask all States south to do the same thing.

I am for exhausting all that patriotism can demand before taking the last step. I would invite, therefore, South Carolina to a conference. I would ask the same of all the other Southern States, so that if the evil has got beyond our control, which God, in his mercy, grant may not be the case, let us not be divided among ourselves—(cheers,)—but, if possible, secure the united coöperation of all the Southern States; and then, in the face of the civilized world, we may justify our action; and, with the wrong all on the other side, we can appeal to the God of battles to aid us in our cause. (Loud applause.) But let us not do anything in which any portion of our people may charge us with rash or hasty action. It is certainly a matter of great importance to tear this Government asunder. You were not sent here for that purpose. I would wish the whole South to be united if this is to be done; and I believe if we pursue the policy which I have indicated, this can be effected.

In this way our sister Southern States can be induced to act with us, and I have but little doubt that the States of New York and Pennsylvania and Ohio, and the other Western States, will compel their Legislatures to recede from their hostile attitude if the others do not. Then with these we would go on without New England if she chose to stay out.

A voice in the assembly—We will kick them out.

Mr. STEPHENS—I would not kick them out. But

if they chose to stay out they might. I think, moreover, that these Northern States being principally engaged in manufactures, would find that they had as much interest in the Union under the Constitution as we, and that they would return to their constitutional duty—this would be my hope. If they should not, and if the Middle States and Western States do not join us, we should at least have an undivided South. I am, as you clearly perceive, for maintaining the Union as it is, if possible. I will exhaust every means thus to maintain it with an equality in it. My principles are these:

First, the maintenance of the honor, the rights, the equality, the security, and the glory of my native State in the Union; but if these cannot be maintained in the Union, then I am for their maintenance, at all hazards, out of it. Next to the honor and glory of Georgia, the land of my birth, I hold the honor and glory of our common country. In Savannah I was made to say by the reporters, who very often make me say things which I never did, that I was first for the glory of the whole country, and next for that of Georgia.

I said the exact reverse of this. I am proud of her history, of her present standing. I am proud even of her motto, which I would have duly respected at the present time by all her sons—Wisdom, Justice, and Moderation. I would have her rights and that of the Southern States maintained now upon these principles. Her position now is just what it was in 1850, with respect to the Southern States. Her platform then has been adopted by most, if not all, the other Southern States. Now I would add but one additional plank to that platform, which I have stated, and one which time has shown to be necessary.

If all this fails, we shall at least have the satisfaction of knowing that we have done our duty and all that patriotism could require.

Mr. Stephens continued for some time on other matters, which are omitted, and then took his seat amidst great applause.

DECLARATION OF CAUSES

WHICH INDUCED THE SECESSION OF SOUTH CAROLINA.

The people of the State of South Carolina in Convention assembled, on the 2d day of April, A. D. 1852, declared that the frequent violations of the Constitution of the United States by the Federal Government, and its encroachments upon the reserved rights of the States, fully justified this State in their withdrawal from the Federal Union; but in deference to the opinions and wishes of the other Slaveholding States, she forbore at that time to exercise this right. Since that time these encroachments have continued to increase, and further forbearance ceases to be a virtue.

And now the State of South Carolina, having resumed her separate and equal place among nations, deems it due to herself, to the remaining United States of America, and to the nations of the world, that she should declare the immediate causes which have led to this act.

In the year 1765, that portion of the British Empire embracing Great Britain undertook to make laws for the Government of that portion composed of the thirteen American Colonies. A struggle for the right of self-government ensued, which resulted, on the 4th of July, 1776, in a Declaration, by the Colonies, "that they are, and of right ought to be, FREE AND INDEPENDENT STATES; and that, as free and independent States, they have full power to levy war, conclude peace, contract alliances, establish commerce, and to do all other acts and things which independent States may of right do."

They further solemnly declared that whenever any "form of government becomes destructive of the ends for which it was established, it is the right of the people to alter or abolish it, and to institute a new government." Deeming the Government of Great Britain to have become destructive of these ends, they declared that the Colonies "are absolved from all allegiance to the British Crown, and that all political connection between them and the State of Great Britain is, and ought to be, totally dissolved."

In pursuance of this Declaration of Independence, each of the thirteen States proceeded to exercise its separate sovereignty; adopted for itself a Constitution, and appointed officers for the administration of government in all its departments —Legislative, Executive and Judicial. For purposes of defence they united their arms and their counsels; and, in 1778, they entered into a League known as the Articles of Confederation, whereby they agreed to intrust the administration of their external relations to a common agent, known as the Congress of the United States, expressly declaring, in the first article, "that each State retains its sovereignty, freedom and independence, and every power, jurisdiction and right which is not, by this Confederation, expressly delegated to the United States in Congress assembled."

Under this Confederation the War of the Revolution was carried on; and on the 3d of September, 1783, the contest ended, and a definite Treaty was signed by Great Britain, in which she acknowledged the Independence of the Colonies in the following terms:

"ARTICLE 1. His Britannic Majesty acknowledges the said United States, viz.: New Hampshire, Massachusetts Bay, Rhode Island and Providence Plantations, Connecticut, New York, New Jersey, Pennsylvania, Delaware, Maryland, Virginia, North Carolina, South Carolina and Georgia, to be FREE, SOVEREIGN, AND INDEPENDENT STATES; that he treats with them as such; and, for himself, his heirs and successors, relinquishes all claims to the government, propriety, and territorial rights of the same and every part thereof."

Thus were established the two great principles asserted by the Colonies, namely, the right of a State to govern itself; and the right of a people to abolish a Government when it becomes destructive of the ends for which it was instituted. And concurrent with the establishment of these principles, was the fact that each Colony became and was recognized by the mother country as a FREE, SOVEREIGN AND INDEPENDENT STATE.

In 1787, Deputies were appointed by the States to revise the articles of Confederation; and on 17th September, 1787, these Deputies recommended, for the adoption of the States, the Articles of Union, known as the Constitution of the United States.

The parties to whom this constitution was submitted were the several sovereign States; they were to agree or disagree, and when nine of them agreed, the compact was to take effect among those concurring; and the General Government, as the common agent, was then to be invested with their authority.

If only nine of the thirteen States had concurred, the other four would have remained as they then were—separate, sovereign States, independent of any of the provisions of the Constitution. In fact, two of the States did not accede to the Constitution until long after it had gone into operation among the other eleven; and during that interval, they each exercised the functions of an independent nation.

By this Constitution, certain duties were imposed upon the several States, and the exercise of certain of their powers was restrained, which necessarily impelled their continued existence as sovereign states. But, to remove all doubt, an amendment was added, which declared that the powers not delegated to the United States by the Constitution, nor prohibited by it to the States, are reserved to the States respectively, or to the people. On the 23d May, 1788, South Carolina, by a Convention of her people, passed an ordinance assenting to this Constitution, and afterwards altered her own Constitution to conform herself to the obligation she had undertaken.

Thus was established, by compact between the States, a Government with defined objects and powers, limited to the express words of the grant. This limitation left the whole remaining mass of power subject to the clause reserving it to the States or the people, and rendered unnecessary any specification of reserved rights. We hold that the

Government thus established is subject to the two great principles asserted in the Declaration of Independence; and we hold further that the mode of its formation subjects it to a third fundamental principle, namely, the law of compact. We maintain that in every compact between two or more parties, the obligation is mutual; that the failure of one of the contracting parties to perform a material part of the agreement, entirely releases the obligation of the other; and that where no arbiter is provided, each party is remitted to his own judgment to determine the fact of failure, with all its consequences.

In the present case, that fact is established with certainty. We assert that fourteen of the States have deliberately refused for years past to fufill their constitutional obligations, and we refer to their own statutes for the proof.

The Constitution of the United States, in its fourth Article, provides as follows:

> "No person held to service or labor in one State under the laws thereof, escaping into another, shall, in consequence of any law or regulation therein, be discharged from such service or labor, but shall be delivered up, on claim of the party to whom such service or labor may be due."

This stipulation was so material to the compact that without it that compact would not have been made. The greater number of the contracting parties held slaves, and they had previously evinced their estimate of the value of such a stipulation by making it a condition in the Ordinance for the government of the territory ceded by Virginia, which obligations, and the laws of the General Government, have ceased to effect the objects of the Constitution. The States of Maine, New Hampshire, Vermont, Massachusetts, Connecticut, Rhode Island, New York, Pennsylvania, Illinois, Indiana, Michigan, Wisconsin, and Iowa, have enacted laws which either nullify the acts of Congress, or render useless any attempt to execute them. In many of these States the fugitive is discharged from the service of labor claimed, and in none of them has the State Government complied with the stipulation made in the Constitution. The State of New Jersey, at an early day, passed a law in conformity with her constitutional obligation; but the current of Anti-Slavery feeling has led her more recently to enact laws which render inoperative the remedies provided by her own laws and by the laws of Congress. In the State of New York even the right of transit for a slave has been denied by her tribunals; and the States of Ohio and Iowa have refused to surrender to justice fugitives charged with murder, and with inciting servile insurrection in the State of

Virginia. Thus the constitutional compact has been deliberately broken and disregarded by the non-slaveholding States; and the consequence follows that South Carolina is released from her obligation.

The ends for which this Constitution was framed are declared by itself to be "to form a more perfect union, to establish justice, insure domestic tranquillity, provide for the common defence, promote the general welfare, and secure the blessings of liberty to ourselves and our posterity."

These ends it endeavored to accomplish by a Federal Government, in which each State was recognized as an equal, and had separate control over its own institutions. The right of property in slaves was recognized by giving to free persons distinct political rights; by giving them the right to represent, and burdening them with direct taxes for, three-fifths of their slaves; by authorizing the importation of slaves for twenty years; and by stipulating for the rendition of fugitives from labor.

We affirm that these ends for which this Government was instituted have been defeated, and the Government itself has been destructive of them by the action of the non-slaveholding States. Those States have assumed the right of deciding upon the propriety of our domestic institutions; and have denied the rights of property established in fifteen of the States and recognized by the Constitution ; they have denounced as sinful the institution of Slavery; they have permitted the open establishment among them of societies, whose avowed object is to disturb the peace of and eloin the property of the citizens of other States. They have encouraged and assisted thousands of our slaves to leave their homes; and those who remain, have been incited by emissaries, books, and pictures, to servile insurrection.

For twenty-five years this agitation has been steadily increasing, until it has now secured to its aid the power of the common Government. Observing the *forms* of the Constitution, a sectional party has found within that article establishing the Executive Department, the means of subverting the Constitution itself. A geographical line has been drawn across the Union, and all the States north of that line have united in the election of a man to the high office of President of the United States whose opinions and purposes are hostile to Slavery. He is to be intrusted with the administration of the common Government, because he has declared that that "Government cannot endure permanently half slave, half free," and that the public mind must rest in the belief that Slavery is in the course of ultimate extinction.

This sectional combination for the subversion of

the Constitution has been aided, in some of the States, by elevating to citizenship persons who, by the supreme law of the land, are incapable of becoming citizens; and their votes have been used to inaugurate a new policy, hostile to the South, and destructive of its peace and safety.

On the 4th of March next this party will take possession of the Government. It has announced that the South shall be excluded from the common territory, that the Judicial tribunal shall be made sectional, and that a war must be waged against Slavery until it shall cease throughout the United States.

The guarantees of the Constitution will then no longer exist; the equal rights of the States will be lost. The Slaveholding States will no longer have the power of self-government, or self-protection, and the Federal Government will have become their enemy.

Sectional interest and animosity will deepen the irritation; and all hope of remedy is rendered vain, by the fact that the public opinion at the North has invested a great political error with the sanctions of a more erroneous religious belief.

We, therefore, the people of South Carolina, by our Delegates in Convention assembled, appealing to the Supreme Judge of the world for the rectitude of our intentions, have solemnly declared that the Union heretofore existing between this State and the other States of North America is dissolved, and that the State of South Carolina has resumed her position among the nations of the world, as a separate and independent state, with full power to levy war, conclude peace, contract alliances, establish commerce, and to do all other acts and things which independent States may of right do.

ORDINANCES OF SECESSION.

SOUTH CAROLINA.

An Ordinance to Dissolve the Union between the State of South Carolina and other States united with her under the compact entitled the Constitution of the United States of America:

We, the people of the State of South Carolina, in Convention assembled, do declare and ordain, and it is hereby declared and ordained, that the ordinance adopted by us in Convention, on the 23d day of May, in the year of our Lord 1788, whereby the Constitution of the United States of America was ratified, and also all Acts and parts of Acts of the General Assembly of this State ratifying the amendments of the said Constitution, are hereby repealed, and that the Union now subsisting between South Carolina and other States, under the name of the United States of America, is hereby dissolved.

The ordinance was taken up and passed by a unanimous vote of 169 members, at a quarter past one o'clock, December 2, 1860.

LOUISIANA.

An Ordinance to dissolve the Union between the State of Louisiana and the other States united with her, under the compact entitled the Constitution of the United States of America:

We, the people of the State of Louisiana, in Convention assembled, do declare and ordain, and it is hereby declared and ordained that the ordinance passed by the State of 22d November, 1807, whereby the Constitution of the United States of America and the amendments of said Constitution were adopted, and all the laws and ordinances by which Louisiana became a member of the Federal Union, be, and the same are hereby repealed and abrogated, and the Union now subsisting between Louisiana and the other States, under the name of the United States of America, is hereby dissolved.

We further declare and ordain, that the State of Louisiana hereby resumes the rights and powers heretofore delegated to the Government of the United States of America, and its citizens are absolved from allegiance to the said Government, and she is in full possession of all the rights and sovereignty that appertain to a free and independent State.

We further declare and ordain, that all rights acquired and vested under the Constitution of the United States, or any act of Congress, or treaty, or under laws of this State not incompatible with this ordinance shall remain in force, and have the same effect as though this ordinance had not passed.

A resolution was reported to the Convention that the following be added to the ordinance:

We, the people of Louisiana, recognize the right of free navigation of the Mississippi River and tributaries by all friendly States bordering thereon, we also recognize the rights of the ingress and egress of the mouths of the Mississippi by all friendly States and Powers, and hereby declare our willingness to enter into stipulations to guarantee the exercise of those rights.

ALABAMA.

An Ordinance to dissolve the Union between the State of Alabama and other States, united under the compact and style of the United States of America.

Whereas, The election of Abraham Lincoln and Hannibal Hamlin to the offices of President and Vice President of the United States of America, by a sectional party, avowedly hostile to the domestic institutions, and peace and security of the people of the State of Alabama, following upon the heels of many and dangerous infractions of the Constitution of the United States, by many of the States and people of the Northern section, is a political wrong of so insulting and menacing a character, as to justify the people of the State of Alabama in the adoption of prompt and decided measures for their future peace and prosperity.

Therefore, be it declared and ordained, by the people of the State of Alabama, in Convention assembled, that the State of Alabama now withdraws from the Union, known as the United States of America, and henceforth ceases to be one of the said United States, and is, and of right ought to be a sovereign independent State.

SEC. 2. And be it further declared and ordained by the people of the State of Alabama in Convention assembled, that all powers over the territories of said State, and over the people thereof, heretofore delegated to the Government of the United States of America, be, and they are hereby, withdrawn from the said Government, and are hereby resumed and vested in the people of the State of Alabama.

And as it is the desire and purpose of the people of Alabama, to meet the slaveholding States of the

South who approve of such a purpose, in order to frame a revisional as a permanent Government, upon the principles of the Government of the United States, be it also resolved by the people of Alabama, in Convention assembled, that the people of the States of Delware, Maryland, Virginia, North Carolina, South Carolina, Florida, Georgia, Mississippi, Louisiana, Texas, Arkansas, Tennessee, Kentucky and Missouri, be and · they are hereby invited to meet the people of the State of Alabama, by their delegates, in convention, on the 4th day of February next, in Montgomery, in the State of Alabama, for the purpose of consultation with each other, as to the most effectual mode of securing concerted, harmonious action in whatever measures may be deemed most desirable for the common peace and security.

And be it further enacted, That the President of this Convention be and he is hereby instructed to transmit forthwith a copy of the foregoing preamble, ordinance and resolutions to the Governors of the several States named in the said resolution.

Done by the people of Alabama, in Convention assembled, at Montgomery, this 11th day of January, 1861.

The preamble, ordinance and resolutions were adopted by Ayes 61, Nays 39.

ARKANSAS.

An Ordinance to dissolve the Union now existing between the State of Arkansas and the other States united with her under the compact entitled "The Constitution of the United States of America."

Whereas, In addition to the well-founded cause of complaint set forth by this Convention in resolutions adopted on the 11th March, A. D. 1861, against the sectional party now in power at Washington City, headed by Abraham Lincoln, he has, in the face of the resolutions passed by this Convention, pledging the State of Arkansas to resist to the last extremity any attempt on the part of such power to coerce any State that seceded from the old Union, proclaimed to the world that war should be waged against such States, until they should be compelled to submit to their rule, and large forces to accomplish this have by this same power been called out, and are now being marshalled to carry out this inhuman design, and longer to submit to such rule or remain in the old Union of the United States would be disgraceful and ruinous to the State of Arkansas:

Therefore, we, the people of the State of Arkansas, in Convention assembled, do hereby declare and ordain, and it is hereby declared and ordained, that the "ordinance and acceptance of compact," passed and approved by the General Assembly of the State of Arkansas on the 18th day of October, A. D. 1836, whereby it was by said General Assembly ordained that, by virtue of the authority invested in said General Assembly, by the provisions of the ordinance adopted by the Convention of delegates assembled at Little Rock for the purpose of forming a Constitution and system of Government for said State, the propositions set forth in "an act supplementary to an act entitled an act for the admission of the State of Arkansas into the Union, and to provide for the due execution of the laws of the United States within the same, and for other purposes, were freely accepted, ratified, and irrevocably confirmed articles of compact and union between the State of Arkansas and the United States," and all other laws, and every other law and ordinance, whereby the State of Arkansas became a member of the Federal Union, be, and the same are hereby in all respects, and for every purpose herewith consistent, repealed, abrogated, and fully set aside; and the union now subsisting between the State of Arkansas and the other States under the name of the United States of America, is hereby forever dissolved.

And we do further hereby declare and ordain that the State of Arkansas hereby resumes to herself all rights and powers heretofore delegated to the Government of the United States of America —that her citizens are absolved from all allegiance to said Government of the United States, and that she is in full possession and exercise of all the rights and sovereignty which appertain to a free and independent State.

We do further ordain and declare that all rights acquired and vested under the Constitution of the United States of America, or of any act or acts of Congress, or treaty, or under any law of this State, and not incompatible with this ordinance, shall remain in full force and effect, in no wise altered or impaired, and have the same effect as if this ordinance had not been passed.

Adopted and passed in open Convention on the 6th day of May, Anno Domini 1861.

ELIAS C. BOUDINOT,
Secretary of the Arkansas State Convention.

NORTH CAROLINA.

WE, the people of the State of North Carolina, in Convention assembled, do declare and ordain, and it is hereby declared and ordained, that the ordinance adopted by the State of North Carolina, in the convention of 1789, whereby the Constitution of the United States was ratified and adopted, and also all acts and parts of acts of the General Assembly, ratifying and adopting amendments to the said Constitution, are hereby repealed, rescinded, and abrogated.

We do further declare and ordain that the Union now subsisting between the State of North Carolina and the other States, under the title of the United States of America, is hereby dissolved, and that the State of North Carolina is in the full possession and exercise of all those rights of sovereignty which belong and appertain to a free and independent State.

Done at Raleigh, 20th day of May, in the year of our Lord 1861.

The following ordinance was also passed:

We, the people of North Carolina, in Convention assembled, do declare and ordain, and it is hereby declared and ordained, that the State of North Carolina does hereby assent to and ratify the Constitution for the Provisional Government of the Confederate States of America, adopted at Montgomery, in the State of Alabama, on the 8th of February, 1861, by the Convention of Delegates from the States of South Carolina, Georgia, Florida,

Alabama, Mississippi, and Louisiana, and that North Carolina will enter into the federal association of States upon the terms therein proposed, when admitted by the Congress or any competent authority of the Confederate States.

Done at Raleigh, 20th day of May, in the year of our Lord 1861.

VIRGINIA.

The following is the "ordinance to repeal the ratification of the Constitution of the United States of America, by the State of Virginia, and to resume all the rights and powers granted under said Constitution," which passed the State Convention on the 17th of April, 1861:

The people of Virginia, in the ratification of the Constitution of the United States of America, adopted by them in Convention, on the 25th day of June, in the year of our Lord one thousand seven hundred and eighty-eight, having declared that the powers granted under the said Constitution were derived from the people of the United States, and might be resumed whensoever the same should be perverted to their injury and oppression, and the Federal Government having perverted said powers, not only to the injury of the people of Virginia, but to the oppression of the Southern slaveholding States;

Now, therefore, we, the people of Virginia, do declare and ordain, that the ordinance adopted by the people of this State in convention on the twenty-fifth day of June, in the year of our Lord one thousand seven hundred and eighty-eight, whereby the Constitution of the United States of America was ratified, and all acts of the General Assembly of this State ratifying or adopting amendments to said Constitution, are hereby repealed and abrogated; that the Union between the State of Virginia and the other States under the Constitution aforesaid is hereby dissolved, and that the State of Virginia is in the full possession and exercise of all the rights of sovereignty which belong and appertain to a free and independent State. And they do further declare that said Constitution of the United States of America is no longer binding on any of the citizens of this State.

This ordinance shall take effect and be an act of this day, when ratified by a majority of the votes of the people of this State, cast at a poll to be taken thereon, on the fourth Thursday in May next, in pursuance of a schedule hereafter to be enacted.

Done in convention in the city of Richmond, on the seventeenth day of April, in the year of our

Lord one thousand eight hundred and sixty-one, and in the eighty-fifth year of the Commonwealth of Virginia.

JNO. L. EUBANK,
Secretary of Convention.

TEXAS.

An Ordinance to dissolve the Union between the State of Texas and the other States under the compact styled the Constitution of the United States of America.

SEC. 1. Whereas, the Federal Government has failed to accomplish the purposes of the compact of Union between these States, in giving protection either to the persons of our people upon an exposed frontier, or to the property of our citizens; and whereas, the action of the Northern States is violative of the compact between the States and the guarantees of the Constitution; and, whereas, the recent developments in federal affairs make it evident that the power of the Federal Government is sought to be made a weapon with which to strike down the interests and property of the people of Texas and her sister slaveholding States, instead of permitting it to be, as was intended—our shield against outrage and aggression—therefore, "We, the people of the State of Texas, by delegates in the

Convention assembled, do declare and ordain that the ordinance adopted by our Convention of delegates on the fourth (4th) day of July, A. D. 1845, and afterwards ratified by us, under which the Republic of Texas was admitted into the Union with other States, and became a party to the compact styled 'The Constitution of the United States of America,' be and is hereby repealed and annulled."

That all the powers which, by the said compact, were delegated by Texas to the Federal Government are resumed. That Texas is of right absolved from all restraints and obligations incurred by said compact, and is a separate sovereign State, and that her citizens and people are absolved from all allegiance to the United States or the Government thereof.

SEC. 2. The ordinance shall be submitted to the people of Texas for their ratification or rejection, by the qualified voters, on the 23d day of February, 1861; and unless rejected by a majority of the votes cast, shall take effect and be in force on and after the 2d day of March, A. D. 1861. Provided, that in the representative district of El Paso said election may be held on the 18th day of February, 1861.

Done by the people of the State of Texas, in convention assembled, at Austin, the 1st day of February, A. D. 1861.

MISSISSIPPI.

ADOPTED JANUARY 9TH, 1861.

THE people of Mississippi, in convention assem bled, do ordain and declare, and it is hereby ordained and declared as follows, to wit.:

That all the laws and ordinances by which the said State of Mississippi became a member of the federal of the United States of America, be, and the same are hereby repealed; and that all obligations on the part of said State, or the people thereof, to observe the same be withdrawn; and that the said State shall hereby resume the rights, functions, and powers, which, by any of said laws and ordinances, where conveyed to the Government of the said United States, and is dissolved from all the obligations, restraints, and duties incurred to the said Federal Union, and shall henceforth be a free, sovereign and independent State.

FLORIDA.

ADOPTED JANUARY 11TH, 1861.

Whereas, All hope of preserving the Union upon terms consistent with the safety and honor of the slaveholding States, has been finally dissipated by the recent indications of the strength of the anti-slavery sentiment of the free States; therefore,

Be it resolved by the people of Florida, in Convention assembled, That it is undoubtedly the right of the several States of the Union, at such times, and for such cause as in the opinion of the people of such State, acting in their sovereign capacity, may be just and proper; and, in the opinion of this Convention, the existing causes are such as to compel Florida to proceed to exercise that right.

We, the people of the State of Florida, in Convention assembled, do solemnly ordain, publish and declare that the State of Florida hereby withdraws herself from the Confederacy of States existing under the name of the United States of America, and from the existing Government of the said States; and that all political connection between her and the Government of the said States ought to be, and the same is hereby totally annulled, and said Union of States dissolved; and the State of Florida is hereby declared a sovereign and independent nation; and that all ordinances heretofore adopted, in so far as they create or recognize said Union, are rescinded; and all laws, or parts of laws, in force in this State, in so far as they recognize or assent to said Union, be and they are hereby repealed.

GEORGIA.

An Ordinance to dissolve the Union between the State of Georgia and other States vnited with her under the compact of Government entitled the Constitution of the United States.

We, the people of the State of Georgia, in Convention assembled, do declare and ordain, and it is hereby declared and ordained, that the ordinances adopted by the people of the State of Georgia in convention in 1788, whereby the Constitution of the United States was assented to, ratified and adopted, and also all acts and parts of acts of the General Assembly ratifying and adopting amendments to the said Constitution, are hereby repealed, rescinded and abrogated.

And we do further declare and ordain that the Union now subsisting between the State of Georgia and other States, under the name of the United States is hereby dissolved, and that the State of Georgia is in full possession and exercise of all those rights of sovereignty which belong and appertain to a free and independent State.

Adopted by a vote of 208 against 89, Jan. 19th, 1861.

SPEECH OF JEFFERSON DAVIS

ON LEAVING THE UNITED STATES SENATE.

I rise for the purpose of announcing to the Senate that I have satisfactory evidence that the State of Mississippi, by solemn ordinance in convention assembled, has declared her separation from the United States. Under these circumstances, of course, my functions terminate here. It has seemed to be proper that I should appear in the Senate and announce that act, and to say something, though very little, upon it. The occasion does not invite me to go into the argument, and my physical condition will not permit it, yet something would seem to be necessary on the part of the State I here represent, on an occasion like this. It is known to Senators who have served here, that I have for many years advocated, as an essential attribute of State sovereignty, the right of a State to secede from the Union. If, therefore, I had not believed there was justifiable cause—if I had thought the State was acting without sufficient provocation—still, under my theory of government, I should have felt bound by her action. I, however, may say I think she had justifiable cause, and I approve of her acts. I conferred with the people before that act was taken, and counselled them that if they could not remain, that they should take the act. I hope none will confound this expression of opinion with the advocacy of the right of a State to remain in the Union, and disregard its constitutional obligations by nullification. Nullification and secession are indeed antagonistic principles. Nullification is the remedy which is to be sought and applied, within the Union, against an agent of the United States, when the agent has violated constitutional obligations, and the State assumes for itself, and appeals to other States to support it. But when the States themselves, and the people of the States, have so acted as to convince us that they will not regard our constitutional rights, then, and then for the first time, arises the question of secession in its practical application. That great man who now reposes with his fathers, who has been so often arraigned for want of fealty to the Union, advocated the doctrine of nullification, because it preserved the Union. It was because of his deep-seated attachment to the Union that Mr. Calhoun advocated the doctrine of nullification, which he claimed would give peace within the limits of the Union, and not disturb it, and only be the means of bringing the agent before the proper tribunal of the States for judgment. Secession belongs to a different class of rights, and is to be justified upon the basis that the States are sovereign. The time has been, and I hope the time will come again, when a better appreciation of our Union will prevent any one denying that each State is a sovereign in its own right. Therefore, I say I concur in the act of my State, and feel bound by it. It is by this confounding of nullification and secession that the name of another great man has been invoked to justify the coercion of a seceding State. The phrase "to execute the law," as used by General Jackson, was applied to a State refusing to obey the laws and still remaining in the Union. I remember well when Massachusetts was arraigned before the Senate. The record of that occasion will show that I said, if Massachusetts, in pursuing the line of steps, takes the last step which separates her from the Union, the right is hers, and I will neither vote one dollar nor one man to coerce her, but I will say to her, "God speed!" Mr. Davis then proceeded to argue that the equality spoken of in the Declaration of Independence was the equality of a class in political rights, referring to the charge against George III.

for inciting insurrection, as proof that it had no reference to the slaves. But we have proclaimed our independence. This is done with no hostility or any desire to injure any section of the country, nor even for our pecuniary benefit, but from the high and solid foundation of defending and protecting the rights we inherited, and transmitting them unshorn to our posterity. I know no hostility to you Senators here, and am sure there is not one of you, whatever may have been the sharp discussion between us, to whom I cannot now say, in the presence of my God, I wish you well. And such is the feeling, I am sure, the people I represent feel towards those whom you represent. I, therefore, feel I but express their desire, when I say I hope and they hope for those peaceful relations with you, though we must part, that may be mutually beneficial to us in the future. There will be peace if you so will it, and you may bring disaster on every part of the country, if you thus will have it. And if you will have it thus, we will invoke the God of our fathers, who delivered them from the paw of the lion, to protect us from the ravages of the bear; and thus putting our trust in God, and our own firm hearts and strong arms, we will vindicate and defend the rights we claim. In the course of my long career, I have met with a great variety of men here, and there have been points of collision between us. Whatever of offence there has been to me, I leave here. I carry no hostile feelings away. Whatever of offence I have given, which has not been redressed, I am willing to say to Senators in this hour of parting, I offer you my apology for any thing I may have done in the Senate; and I go thus released from obligation, remembering no injury I have received, and having discharged what I deem the duty of man, to offer the only reparation at this hour for every injury I have ever inflicted.

[As the Senators from Florida, Alabama and Mississippi were about to retire from the Senate, all the Democratic Senators crowded around them and shook hands with them. Messrs. Hale and Cameron were the only Republican Senators that did so.]

AFRICAN SLAVERY,

THE CORNER-STONE OF THE SOUTHERN CONFEDERACY.

A SPEECH BY HON. ALEXANDER H. STEPHENS, VICE-PRESIDENT OF THE CONFEDERATE STATES OF AMERICA, DELIVERED AT THE ATHENEUM, SAVANNAH, MARCH 22, 1861.

MR. MAYOR AND GENTLEMEN OF THE COMMITTEE, AND FELLOW-CITIZENS—For this reception you will please accept my most profound and sincere thanks. The compliment is doubtless intended as much, or more perhaps, in honor of the occasion, and my public position in connection with the great events now crowding upon us, than to me personally and individually. It is, however, none the less appreciated on that account. We are in the midst of one of the greatest epochs in our history. The last ninety days will mark one of the most memorable eras in the history of modern civilization.

[There was a general call from the outside of the building for the speaker to go out; that there were more outside than in. The Mayor rose and requested silence at the doors; said

Mr. Stephens's health would not permit him to speak in the open air. Mr. Stephens said he would leave it to the audience whether he should proceed indoors or out. There was a general cry indoors, as the ladies—a large number of whom were present—could not hear outside. Mr. Stephens said that the accommodation of the ladies would determine the question, and he would proceed where he was. At this point the uproar and clamor outside were greater still for the speaker to go out on the steps. This was quieted by Col Lawton, Col. Foreman, Judge Jackson, and Mr. J. W. Owens, going out and stating the facts of the case to the dense mass of men, women, and children who were outside, and entertaining them in short, brief speeches, Mr. Stephens all this time quietly sitting down until the furor subsided.]

Mr. Stephens rose and said—When perfect quiet is restored I shall proceed. I cannot speak as long as there is any noise or confusion. I shall take my time. I feel as though I could spend the night with you, if necessary. (Loud applause.) I very much regret that every one who desires cannot hear what I have to say, not that I have any display to make, or anything very entertaining to present; but such views as I have to give I wish *all*, not only in this city, but in this State, and throughout our Confederated Republic, could hear, who have a desire to hear them.

I was remarking that we were passing through one of the greatest revolutions in the annals of the world. Seven States have, within the last three months, thrown off an old government, and formed a new. This revolution has been signally marked, up to this time, by the fact of its having been accomplished without the loss of a single drop of blood. (Applause.) This new constitution, or form of government, constitutes the subject to which your attention will be partly invited.

In reference to it, I make this first general remark: It amply secures all our ancient rights, franchises, and privileges. All the great principles of Magna Charta are retained in it. No citizen is deprived of life, liberty, or property but by the judgment of his peers, under the laws of the land. The great principle of religious liberty, which was the honor and pride of the old Constitution, is still maintained and secured. All the essentials of the old Constitution, which have endeared it to the hearts of the American people, have been preserved and perpetuated. (Applause.) Some changes have been made; of these I shall speak presently. Some of these I should have preferred not to have been made, but these perhaps meet the cordial approbation of a majority of this audience, if not an overwhelming majority of the people of the Confederacy. Of them, therefore, I will not speak. But other important changes do meet my cordial approbation. They form great improvements on the old Constitution. So, taking the whole new Constitution, I have no hesitancy in giving it as my judgment, that it is decidedly better than the old. (Applause.)

Allow me briefly to allude to some of these improvements. The question of building up class interests, or fostering one branch of industry to the prejudice of another, under the exercise of the revenue power, which gave us so much trouble under the old Constitution, is put at rest forever under the new. We allow the imposition of no duty with a view of giving advantages to one class of persons, in any trade or business, over those of another. All, under our system, stand upon the same broad principles of perfect equality. Honest labor and enterprise are left free and unrestricted in whatever pursuit they may be engaged. This subject came well nigh causing a rupture of the old Union, under the lead of the gallant Palmetto State, which lies on our border, in 1833.

This old thorn of the tariff, which occasioned the cause of so much irritation in the old body politic, is removed forever from the new. (Applause.) Again, the subject of internal improvements, under the power of Congress to regulate commerce, is put at rest under our system. The power claimed by construction under the old Constitution was, at least, a doubtful one—it rested solely upon construction. We, of the South, generally apart from considerations of constitutional principles, opposed its exercise upon grounds of expediency and justice. Notwithstanding this opposition, millions of money in the common treasury had been drawn for such purposes. Our opposition sprung from no hostily to commerce, or all necessary aids for facilitating it. With us it was simply a question upon *whom* the burden should fall. In Georgia, for instance, we had done as much for the cause of internal improvements as any other portion of the country, according to population and means. We have stretched out lines of railroads from the seaboard to the mountains; dug down the hills and filled up the valleys at a cost of not less than $25,000,000. All this was done to open up an outlet for our products of the interior, and those to the west of us, to reach the marts of the world. No State was in greater need of such facilities than Georgia, but we had not asked that these works should be made by appropriations out of the common Treasury. The cost of the grading, the superstructure and equipments of our roads was borne by those who entered upon the enterprise. Nay, more, not only the cost of the iron, no small item in the aggregate cost, was borne in the same way, but we were compelled to pay into the common Treasury several millions of dollars for the privilege of importing the iron, after the price was paid for it abroad. What justice was there in taking this money, which our people paid into the common Treasury on the importation of our iron, and applying it to the improvement of rivers and harbors elsewhere?

The true principle is, to subject commerce of every locality to whatever burdens may be necessary to facilitate it. If Charleston harbor needs improvement, let the commerce of Charleston bear the burden. If the mouth of the Savannah River has to be cleared out, let the sea-going navigation which is benefitted by it bear the burden. So with the mouths of the Alabama and Mississippi rivers. Just as the products of the interior, our cotton, wheat, corn, and other articles have to bear the necessary rates of frieght over our railroads to reach the seas. This is again the broad principle of perfect equality and justice. (Applause.) And it is specially held forth and established in our new Constitution.

Another feature to which I will allude is, that the new Constitution provides that cabinet ministers and heads of departments shall have the privilege of seats upon the floor of the Senate and House of Representatives—shall have the right to participate in the debates and discussions upon the various subjects of administration. I should have preferred that this provision should have gone further, and allowed the President to select his constitutional advisers from the Senate and House of Representatives. That would have conformed entirely to the practice in the

British Parliament, which, in my judgment, is one of the wisest provisions in the British Parliament. It is the only feature that saves that government. It is that which gives it stability in its facility to change its administration. Ours, as it is, is a great approximation to the right principle.

Under the old Constitution a Secretary of the Treasury, for instance, had no opportunity, save by his annual reports, of presenting any scheme or plan of finance or other matter. He had no opportunity of explaining, expounding, enforcing, or defending his views of policy; his only resort was through the medium of an organ. In the British Parliament the premier brings in his budget, and stands before the nation responsible for its every item. If it is indefensible, he falls before the attacks upon it, as he ought to. This will now be the case, to a limited extent, under our system. Our heads of departments can speak for themselves and the administration, in behalf of its entire policy, without resorting to the indirect and highly objectionable medium of a newspaper. It is to be greatly hoped that under our system we shall never have what is known as a government organ. (Rapturous applause.)

[A noise again arose from the clamor of the crowd outside, who wished to hear Mr. Stephens, and for some moments interrupted him. The Mayor rose and called on the police to preserve order. Quiet being restored, Mr. S. proceeded.]

Another change in the Constitution relates to the length of the tenure of the Presidential office. In the new Constitution it is six years instead of four, and the President rendered inelligible for re-election. This is certainly a decidedly conservative change. It will remove from the incumbent all temptation to use his office or exert the powers confided to him for any objects of personal ambition. The only incentive to that higher ambition which should move and actuate one holding such high trusts in his hands will be the good of the people, the advancement, prosperity, happiness, safety, honor, and true glory of the Confederacy. (Applause.)

But not to be tedious in enumerating the numerous changes for the better, allow me to allude to one other—though last, not least: The new Constitution has put at rest, *forever*, all agitating questions relating to our peculiar institution—African slavery as it exists among us—the proper *status* of the negro in our form of civilization. This was the immediate cause of the late rupture and present revolution. Jefferson, in his forecast, had anticipated this, as the "rock upon which the old Union would split." He was right. What was conjecture with him is now a realized fact. But whether he comprehended the great truth upon which that rock *stood* and *stands*, may be doubted. The prevailing ideas entertained by him and most of the leading statesmen at the time of the formation of the old Constitution were, that the enslavement of the African was in violation of the laws of nature; that it was wrong in *principle*, socially, morally, and politically. It was an evil they knew not well how to deal with, but the general opinion of the men of that day was that, somehow or other, in the order of Providence, the institution would be evanescent and pass away. This idea, though not incorporated in the Constitution, was the prevailing idea at the time. The Constitution, it is true, secured every essential guaranty to the institution while it should last, and hence no argument can be justly used against the constitutional guarantees thus secured, because of the common sentiment of the day. Those ideas, however, were fundamentally wrong. They rested upon the assumption of the equality of races. This was an error. It was a sandy foundation, and the idea of a government built upon it; when the "storm came and the wind blew, it *fell*."

Our new government is founded upon exactly the opposite idea; its foundations are laid, its cornerstone rests upon the great truth that the negro is not equal to the white man. That slavery—subordination to the superior race—is his natural and moral condition. (Applause.)

This, our new government, is the first in the history of the world based upon this great physical, philosophical, and moral truth. This truth has been slow in the process of its development, like all other truths in the various departments of science. It has been so even among us. Many who hear me, perhaps, can recollect well that this truth was not generally admitted even within their day. The errors of the past generation still clung to many as late as twenty years ago. Those at the North who still cling to these errors, with a zeal above knowledge, we justly denominate fanatics. All fanaticism springs from an aberration of the mind—from a defect in reasoning. It is a species of insanity. One of the most striking characteristics of insanity, in many instances, is forming correct conclusions from fancied or erroneous premises; so with the anti-slavery fanatics; their conclusions are right, if their premises are. They assume that the negro is equal, and hence conclude that he is entitled to equal privileges and rights with the white man. If their premises were correct, their conclusion would be logical and just; but their premise being wrong, their whole argument fails. I recollect once of having heard a gentleman from one of the Northern

States, of great power and ability, announce in the House of Representatives, with imposing effect, that we of the South would be compelled, ultimately, to yield upon this subject of slavery; that it was as impossible to war successfully against a principle in politics, as it was in physics or mechanics. That the principle would ultimately prevail. That we, in maintaining slavery as it exists with us, were warring against a principle, a principle founded in nature, the principle of the equality of man. The reply I made to him was, that upon his own grounds we should succeed, and that he and his associates in their crusades against our institutions, would ultimately fail. The truth announced that it was as impossible to war successfully against a principle in politics as in physics and mechanics, I admitted, but told him that it was he and those acting with him who were warring against a principle. They were attempting to make things equal which the Creator had made unequal.

In the conflict thus far, success has been on our side, complete throughout the length and breadth of the Confederate States. It is upon this, as I have stated, our social fabric is firmly planted, and I can not permit myself to doubt the ultimate success of a full recognition of this principle throughout the civilized and enlightened world.

As I have stated, the truth of this principle may be slow in development, as all truths are, and ever have been, in the various branches of science. It was so with the principles announced by Galileo; it was so with Adam Smith and his principles of political economy. It was so with Harvey and his theory of the circulation of the blood. It is stated that not a single one of the medical profession, living at the time of the announcement of the truths made by him, admitted them. Now, they are universally acknowledged. May we not, therefore, look with confidence to the ultimate universal acknowledgment of the truths upon which our system rests? It is the first government ever instituted upon principles in strict conformity to nature, and the ordination of Providence, in furnishing the materials of human society. Many governments have been founded upon the principle of the enslavement of certain classes; but the classes thus enslaved were of the same race and in violation of the laws of nature. Our system commits no such violation of nature's laws. The negro by nature, or by the curse against Canaan, is fitted for that condition which he occupies in our system. The architect, in the construction of buildings, lays the foundation with proper materials—the granite—then comes the brick or the marble. The substratum of our society is made of the material fitted by nature for it, and by experience we know that it is best not only for the superior, but for the inferior race that it should be so. It is, indeed, in conformity with the ordinance of the Creator. It is not for us to inquire into the wisdom of His ordinances or to question them. For His own purposes He has made one race to differ from another, as He has made "one star to differ from another in glory."

The great objects of humanity are best attained, when conformed to His laws and decrees, in the formation of governments as well as in all things else. Our Confederacy is founded upon principles in strict conformity with these laws. This stone which was rejected by the first builders, "is become the chief stone of the corner" in our new edifice. (Applause.)

I have been asked, what of the future? It has been apprehended by some that we would have arrayed against us the civilized world. I care not who or how many they may be, when we stand upon the eternal principles of truth we are obliged and must triumph. (Immense applause.)

Thousands of people who begin to understand these truths are not yet completely out of the shell. They do not see them in their length and breadth. We hear much of the civilization and Christianization of the barbarous tribes of Africa. In my judgment, those ends will never be attained, but by first teaching them the lesson taught to Adam, that "in the sweat of thy brow shalt thou eat bread" (applause), and teaching them to work, and feed, and clothe themselves. But to pass on: some have propounded the inquiry, whether it is practicable for us to go on with the Confederacy without further accessions? Have we the means and ability to maintain nationality among the powers of the earth? On this point I would barely say, that as anxiously as we all have been and are for the Border States, with institutions similar with ours, to join us, still we are abundantly able to maintain our position, even if they should ultimately make up their minds not to cast their destiny with ours. That they ultimately will join us—be compelled to do it—is my confident belief, but we can get on very well without them, even if they should not.

We have all the essential elements of a high national career. The idea has been given out at the North, and even in the Border States, that we are too small and too weak to maintain a separate nationality. This is a great mistake. In extent of territory we embrace 564,000 square miles and upwards. This is upward of 200,000 square miles more than was included within the limits of the original thirteen States. It is an area of country more than double the territory of France or the Austrian Empire. France, in round numbers, has but 212,000 square miles. Austria, in round numbers, has 248,000 square miles. Ours is greater than both combined. It is greater than all France, Spain, Portugal, and Great Britain, including England, Ireland, and Scotland together. In population we have upward of eight millions, according to the census of 1860; this includes white and black. The entire population, including white and black, of the original thirteen States, was less than 4,000,000 in 1790, and still less in '76, when the independence of our fathers was achieved. If they, with a less population, dared to maintain their independence against the greatest power on earth, shall we have any apprehension of maintaining ours now?

In point of material wealth and resources we are greatly in advance of them. The taxable property of the Confederate States can not be less than $22,000,000,000. This, I think, I venture but little in saying, may be considered as five times more than the colonies possessed at the time they achieved their independence. Georgia alone possessed last year, according to the report of our Comptroller-General, $672,000,000 of taxable property. The debts of the seven Confederate States sum up, in the aggregate, less than $18,000,000; while the existing debts of the other of the late United States sum up, in the aggregate, the enormous amount of $174,000,000. This is without taking into the account the heavy city debts, corporation debts, and railroad debts, which press, and will continue to press, a heavy, incubus upon the resources of those States. These debts, added to others, make a sum total not much under $500,000,000. With such an area of territory —with such an amount of population—with a climate and soil unsurpassed by any on the face of the earth—with such resources already at our command—with productions which control the commerce of the world, who can entertain any apprehensions as to our success, whether others join us or not?

It is true, I believe, I state but the common sentiment, when I declare my earnest desire that the Border States should join us. The differences of opinion that existed among us anterior to secession related more to the policy in securing that result by coöperation than from any difference upon the ultimate security we all looked to in common.

These differences of opinion were more in reference to policy than principle, and as Mr. Jefferson said in his inaugural, in 1801, after the heated contest preceding his election, there might be differences in opinion without differences in principle, and that all, to some extent, had been Federalists and all Republicans; so it may now be said of us, that whatever differences of opinion as to the best policy in having a coöperation with our border sister Slave States, if the worst comes to the worst, that as we were all coöperationists, we are all now for independence, whether they come or not. (Continued applause.)

In this connection I take this occasion to state that I was not without grave and serious apprehension, that if the worst came to the worst, and cutting loose from the old government would be the only remedy for our safety and security, it would be attended with much more serious ills than it has been as yet. Thus far we have seen none of those incidents which usually attend revolutions. No such material as such convulsions usually throw up has been seen. Wisdom, prudence, and patriotism have marked every step of our progress thus far. This augurs well for the future, and it is a matter of sincere gratification to me, that I am enabled to make the declaration of the men I met in the Congress at Montgomery (I may be pardoned for saying this), an abler, wiser—a more conservative, deliberate, determined, resolute, and patriotic body of men I never met in my life. (Great applause.)

Their works speak for them; the Provisional Government speaks for them; the Constitution of the permanent Government will be a lasting monument of their worth, merit, and statesmanship. (Applause.)

But to return to the question of the future. What is to be the result of this revolution?

Will everything, commenced so well, continue as it has begun? In reply to this anxious inquiry, I can only say it all depends upon ourselves. A young man starting out in life on his majority, with health, talent, and ability, under a favoring Providence, may be said to be the architect of his own fortunes. His destinies are in his own hands. He may make for himself a name of honor or dishonor, according to his own acts. If he plants himself upon truth, integrity, honor, and uprightness, with industry, patience, and energy, he cannot fail of success. So it is with us; we are a young Republic, just entering upon the arena of nations; we will be the architect of our own fortunes. Our destiny, under Providence, is in our own hands. With wisdom, prudence, and statesmanship on the part of our public men, and intelligence, virtue, and patriotism on the part of the people, success, to the full measures of our most sanguine hopes, may be looked for. But if we become divided—if schisms arise—if dissensions spring up—if factions are engendered—if party spirit, nourished by unholy personal ambition, shall rear its hydra head, I have no good to prophesy for you. Without intelligence, virtue, integrity, and patriotism on the part of the people, no republic or representative government can be durable or stable.

We have intelligence, and virtue, and patriotism. All that is required is to cultivate and perpetuate these. Intelligence will not do without virtue. France was a nation of philosophers. These philosophers became Jacobins. They lacked that virtue, that devotion to moral principle, and that patriotism which is essential to good government. Organized upon principles of perfect justice and right—seeking amity and friendship with all other powers—I see no obstacle in the way of our upward and onward progress. Our growth, by accessions from other States, will depend greatly upon whether we present to the world, as I trust we shall, a better government than that to which they belong. If we do this, North Carolina, Tennessee, and Arkansas can not hesitate long; neither can Virginia, Kentucky, and Missouri. They will necessarily gravitate to us by an imperious law. We made ample provision in our Constitution for the admission of other States; it is more guarded, and wisely so, I think, than the old

Constitution on the same subject, but not too guarded to receive them as fast as it may be proper. Looking to the distant future, and, perhaps, not very distant either, it is not beyond the range of possibility, and even probability, that all the great States of the Northwest shall gravitate this way as well as Tennessee, Kentucky, Missouri, Arkansas, etc. Should they do so, our doors are wide enough to receive them, but not until they are ready to assimilate with us in principle.

The process of disintegration in the old Union may be expected to go on with almost absolute certainty. We are now the nucleus of a growing power, which, if we are true to ourselves, our destiny, and high mission, will become the controlling power on this continent. To what extent accession will go on in the process of time, or where it will end, the future will determine. So far as it concerns States of the old Union, they will be upon no such principle of *reconstruction* as now spoken of, but upon *reorganization* and new assimilation. (Loud applause.) Such are some of the glimpses of the future as I catch them.

But at first we must necessarily meet with the inconveniences, and difficulties, and embarrassments incident to all changes of government. These will be felt in our postal affairs and changes in the channel of trade. These inconveniences, it is to be hoped, will be but temporary, and must be borne with patience and forbearance.

As to whether we shall have war with our late confederates, or whether all matters of differences between us shall be amicably settled, I can only say that the prospect for a peaceful adjustment is better, so far as I am informed, than it has been.

The prospect of war is at least not so threatening as it has been. The idea of coercion shadowed forth in President Lincoln's Inaugural seems not to be followed up thus far so vigorously as was expected. Fort Sumter, it is believed, will soon be evacuated. What course will be pursued toward Fort Pickens and the other forts on the Gulf, is not well understood. It is to be greatly desired that all of them should be surrendered. Our object is *Peace*, not only with the North, but with the world. All matters relating to the public property, public liabilities of the Union when we were members of it, we are ready and willing to adjust and settle, upon the principles of right, equality and good faith. War can be of no more benefit to the North than to us. The idea of coercing us, or subjugating us, is utterly preposterous. Whether the intention of evacuating Fort Sumter is to be received as an evidence of a desire for a peaceful solution of our difficulties with the United States, or the result of necessity, I will not undertake to say. I would fain hope the former. Rumors are afloat, however, that it is the result of necessity. All I can say to you, therefore, on that point is, keep your armor bright and your powder dry. (Enthusiastic applause.)

The surest way to secure peace is to show your ability to maintain your rights. The principles and position of the present Administration of the United States—the Republican party—present some puzzling questions. While it is a fixed principle with them never to allow the increase of a foot of slave territory, they seem to be equally determined not to part with an inch "of the accursed soil." Notwithstanding their clamor against the institution, they seem to be equally opposed to getting more, or letting go what they have got. They were ready to fight on the accession of Texas, and are equally ready to fight now on her secession. Why is this? How can this strange paradox be accounted for? There seems to be but one rational solution, and that is, notwithstanding their professions of humanity, they are disinclined to give up the benefits they derive from slave labor. Their philanthropy yields to their interest. The idea of enforcing the laws has but one object, and that is the collection of the taxes raised by slave labor to swell the fund necessary to meet their heavy appropriations. The spoils is what they are after, though they come from the labor of the slave. (Continued applause.)

Mr. STEPHENS reviewed at some length the extravagance and profligacy of appropriations by the Congress of the United States for several years past, and in this connection took occasion to allude to another one of the great improvements in our new Constitution, which is a clause prohibiting Congress from appropriating any money from the Treasury except by a two-thirds vote, unless it be for some object which the Executive may say is necessary to carry on the Government.

When it is thus asked for and estimated, he continued, the majority may appropriate. This was a new feature.

Our fathers had guarded the assessment of taxes by insisting that representation and taxation should should go together. This was inherited from the mother country—England. It was one of the prin-principles upon which the Revolution had been fought. Our fathers also provided in the old Constitution that all appropriation bills should originate in the Representative branch of Congress; but our new Constitution went a step further, and guarded not only the pockets of the people, but also the public money, after it was taken from their pockets.

He alluded to the difficulties and embarrassments which seemed to surround the question of a peaceful solution of the controversy with the old Government. How can it be done? is perplexing many minds. The President seems to think that he cannot recognize our independence, nor can he, with and by the advice of the Senate, do so. The Constitution makes no such provision. A general convention of all the States has been suggested by some. Without proposing to solve the difficulty, he barely made the following suggestions:

That as the admission of States by Congress under the Constitution was an act of legislation, and in the nature of a contract or compact between the States admitted and the others admitting, why should not this contract or compact be regarded as of like character with all other civil contracts—liable to be rescinded by mutual agreement of both parties? The seceding States have rescinded it on their part. Why can not the whole question be settled, if the North desire peace, simply by the Congress, in both branches, with the concurrence of the President, giving their consent to the separation, and a recognition of our independence? This he merely offered as a suggestion, as one of the ways in which it might be done with much less violence to constructions of the Constitution than many other acts of that Government. (Applause.) The difficulty has to be solved in some way or other--this may be regarded as a fixed fact.

Several other points were alluded to by Mr. S., particularly as to the policy of the new Government toward foreign nations and our commercial relations with them. Free trade, as far as practicable, would be the policy of this Government. No higher duties would be imposed on foreign importation than would be necessary to support the Government upon the strictest economy.

In olden times the olive branch was considered the emblem of peace. We will send to the nations of the earth another and far more potential emblem of the same—the Cotton Plant. The present duties were levied with a view of meeting the present necessities and exigencies, in preparation for war, if need be; but if we had peace—and he hoped we might—and trade should resume its proper course, a duty of ten per cent. upon foreign importations, it was thought, might be sufficient to meet the expenditures of the Government. If some articles should be left on the free list, as they now are, such as breadstuffs, etc., then, of course, duties upon others would have to be higher—but in no event to an extent to embarrass trade and commerce. He concluded in an earnest appeal for union and harmony, on the part of all the people, in support of the common cause, in which we are all enlisted, and upon the issues of which such great consequences depend.

If, said he, we are true to ourselves, true to our cause, true to our destiny, true to our high mission, in presenting to the world the highest type of civilization ever exhibited by man, there will be found in our lexicon no such word as Fail.

Mr. STEPHENS took his seat amid a burst of enthusiasm and applause such as the Atheneum has never displayed within its walls within "the recollection of the oldest inhabitant."

ROBERT TOOMBS' ADDRESS,

TO THE PEOPLE OF GEORGIA,

TELEGRAPHED FROM WASHINGTON, DEC. 23, 1860.

I CAME here to secure your constitutional rights, and to demonstrate to you that you can get no guarantee for those rights from your Northern confederates. The whole subject was referred to a Committee of Thirteen in the Senate. I was appointed on the Committee, and accepted the trust. I submitted propositions, which, so far from receiving decided support from a single member of the Republican party of the Committee, were all treated with derision or contempt. A vote was then taken in the Committee on amendments to the Constitution proposed by Hon. J. J. Crittenden, and each and all of them were voted against unanimously by the Black Republican members of the Committee. In addition to these facts, a majority of the Black Republican members of the Committee declared distinctly that they had no guarantees to offer, which was silently acquiesced in by the other members. The Black Republican members of this Committee of Thirteen are representative men of the party and section, and, to the extent of my information, truly represent them.

The Committee of Thirty-three on Friday adjourned for a week, without coming to any vote, after solemnly pledging themselves to vote on all the propositions then before them on that day. It is controlled by the Black Republicans, your enemies, who only seek to amuse you with delusive hope until your election, that you may defeat the friends of secession. If you are deceived by them, it shall not be my fault. I have put the test fairly and frankly. It is decisive against you now. I tell you, upon the faith of a true man, that all further looking to the North for security for your constitutional rights in the Union ought to be instantly abandoned. It is fraught with nothing but ruin to yourselves and your posterity. Secession by the 4th day of March next should be thundered from the ballot box by the unanimous vote of Georgia on the 2d day of January next. Such a voice will be your best guarantee for liberty, security, tranquillity, and glory.

R. Toombs.

THE CONSTITUTION

OF THE

CONFEDERATE STATES OF AMERICA.

WE, the people of the Confederate States, each State acting in its sovereign and independent character, in order to form a permanent Federal Government, establish justice, insure domestic tranquillity, and secure the blessings of liberty to ourselves and our posterity, invoking the favor and guidance of Almighty God, do ordain and establish this Constitution for the Confederate States of America.

ARTICLE I.

§ 1. All Legislative powers herein delegated shall be vested in a Congress of the Confederate States, which shall consist of a Senate and House of Representatives.

§ 2. The House of Representatives shall be chosen every second year by the people of the several States, and the electors in each State shall be citizens of the Confederate States, and have the qualifications requisite for electors of the most numerous branch of the State Legislature; but no person of foreign birth, not a citizen of the Confederate States, shall be allowed to vote for any officer, civil or political, State or Federal.

2d. No person shall be a representative who shall not have attained the age of twenty-five years, and be a Citizen of the Confederate States, and who shall not, when elected, be an inhabitant of that State in which he shall be chosen.

3d. Representatives and direct taxes shall be apportioned among the several States which may be included within this Confederacy, according to their respective numbers, which shall be determined by adding to the whole number of free persons, including those bound to service for a term of years, and excluding Indians not taxed, three-fifths of all slaves. The actual enumeration shall be made within three years after the first meeting of Congress of the Confederate States, and within every subsequent term of ten years, in such manner as they shall by law direct. The number of representatives shall not exceed one for every fifty thousand, but each State shall have at least one representative, and until such enumeration shall be made, the State of South Carolina shall be entitled to choose six, the State of

Georgia ten, the State of Alabama nine, the State of Florida two, the State of Mississippi seven, the State of Louisiana six, and the State of Texas six.

4th. When vacancies happen in the representation of any State, the executive authority thereof shall issue writs of election to fill such vacancies.

5th. The House of Representatives shall choose their speaker and other officers, and shall have the sole power of impeachment, except that any judicial or other federal officer, resident and acting solely within the limits of any State, may be impeached by a vote of two-thirds of both branches of the legislature thereof.

§ 3. The Senate of the Confederate States shall be composed of two senators from each State, chosen for six years by the legislature thereof at the regular session next immediately preceding the commencement of the term of service, and each senator shall have one vote.

2d. Immediately after they shall be assembled in consequence of the first election, they shall be divided as equally as may be into three classes. The seats of the senators of the first class shall be vacated at the expiration of the second year; of the second class, at the expiration of the fourth year; and of the third class, at the expiration of the sixth year—so that one third may be chosen every second year—and if vacancies happen by resignation or otherwise during the recess of the legislature of any State, the executive may make temporary appointments until the next meeting of the legislature, which shall then fill such vacancies.

3d. No person shall be a senator who shall not have attained the age of thirty years and be a citizen of the Confederate States, and who shall not when elected be an inhabitant of the State for which he shall be chosen.

4th. The Vice-President of the Confederate States shall be President of the Senate, but shall have no vote, unless they be equally divided.

5th. The Senate shall choose their other officers, and also a president (*pro tempore*) in the absence of the Vice-President, or when he shall exercise the office of President of the Confederate States.

6th. The Senate shall have sole power to try all impeachments. When sitting for that purpose, they shall be on oath or affirmation. When the President of the Confederate States is tried, the chief justice shall preside, and no person shall be convicted without the concurrence of two-thirds of the members present.

7th. Judgment in cases of impeachment shall not extend further than removal from office and disqualification to hold and enjoy any office of honor, trust, or profit under the Confederate States; but the party convicted shall nevertheless be liable to, and subject to, indictment, trial, judgment and punishment, according to law.

§ 4. The times, places, and manner of holding elections for senators and representatives shall be prescribed in each State by the legislature thereof, subject to the provisions of this constitution; but the Congress may at any time, by law, make or alter such regulations, except as to the times and places of choosing senators.

2d. The Congress shall assemble at least once in every year, and such meetings shall be on the first Monday in December, unless they shall by law appoint a different day.

§ 5. Each house shall be judge of the elections, returns, and qualifications of its own members, and a majority of each shall constitute a quorum to do business; but a smaller number may adjourn from day to day, and may be authorized to compel the attendance of absent members in such manner and under such penalties as each house may provide.

2d. Each house may determine the rules of its proceedings, punish its members for disorderly behaviour, and with the concurrence of two-thirds of the whole number expel a member.

3d. Each house shall keep a journal of its proceedings, and from time to time publish the same, excepting such parts as may in its judgment require secresy, and the ayes and nays of the members of either house on any question shall, at the desire of one-fifth of those present, be entered on the journal.

4th. Neither house, during the session of Congress, shall, without the consent of the other, adjourn for more than three days, nor to any other place than that in which the two houses shall be sitting.

§ 6. The senators and representatives shall receive a compensation for their services to be ascertained by law, and paid out of the Treasury of the Confederate States. They shall in all cases, except treason and breach of the peace, be privileged from arrest during their attendance at the session of their respective houses, and in going to and from the same, and for any speech or debate in either house they shall not be questioned in any other place.

2d. No senator or representative shall, during the time for which he was elected, be appointed to any civil office under the authority of the Confederate States which shall have been created, or the emoluments whereof shall have been increased during such time, and no person holding office under the Confederate States shall be a member of either house during his continuance in office. But Congress may by law grant to the principal officer in each of the executive departments a seat upon the floor of either house with the privilege of discussing any measure appertaining to his department.

§ 7. All bills for raising revenue shall originate in the House of Representatives; but the Senate may propose or concur with amendments as on other bills.

2d. Every bill which shall have passed both houses shall, before it becomes a law, be presented to the President of the Confederate States; if he approve, he shall sign it; but if not, he will return it with his objections to that house in which it shall have originated, who shall enter the objections at large on their journal, and proceed to reconsider it. If, after such reconsiderations, two-thirds of that house shall agree to pass the bill, it shall be sent, together with the objections to the other house, by which it shall be likewise reconsidered, and if approved by two-thirds of that house, it shall become a law; but in all such cases the votes of both houses shall be determined by ayes and nays, and the names of the persons voting for and against the bill shall be entered on the journal of each house respectively. If any bill shall not be returned by the President within ten days (Sundays excepted) after it shall have been presented to him, the same shall be a law in like manner as if he had signed it, unless the Congress, by their adjournment, prevent its return; in which case it shall not be a law. The President may approve any appropriation and disapprove any other appropriation in the same bill; in such case he shall, in signing the bill, designate the appropriations disapproved, and shall return a copy of such appropriations, with his objections, to the house in which the bill shall have originated, and the same proceedings shall then be had as in case of other bills disapproved by the President.

3d. Every order, resolution, or vote to which the concurrence of both houses may be necessary (except on questions of adjournment) shall be presented to the President of the Confederate States, and before the same shall take effect, shall be approved by him, or, being disapproved by him, may be repassed by two-thirds of both houses, according to the rules and limitations prescribed in case of a bill.

§ 8. The Congress shall have power:

1st. To lay and collect taxes, duties, imposts, and excises for revenue necessary to pay the debts, provide for common defence, and carry on the Government of the Confederate States; but no bounties shall be granted from the treasury, nor shall any duties or taxes on importations from foreign nations be laid to promote or foster any branch of industry, and all duties, imports, and excises shall be uniform throughout the Confederate States.

2d. To borrow money on the credit of the Confederate States.

3d. To regulate commerce with foreign nations and among the several States, and with the Indian tribes; but neither this nor any other clause contained in the constitution shall be construed to delegate the power to Congress to appropriate money for any internal improvement intended to facilitate commerce, except for the purpose of furnishing lights, beacons, and buoys, and other aids to navigation upon the coasts, and the improvement of harbors, and the moveing of obstructions in river navigation, in all which cases such duties shall be laid on the navigation facilitated thereby as may be necessary to pay the costs and expenses thereof.

4th. To establish uniform laws of naturalization, and uniform laws on the subject of bankruptcies throughout the Confederate States; but no law of Congress shall discharge any debt contracted before the passage of the same.

5th. To coin money, regulate the value thereof, and of foreign coin, and fix the standard of weights and measures.

6th. To provide for the punishment of counterfeiting the securities and current coin of the Confederate States.

7th. To establish post offices and post routes; but

the expenses of the post office department after the first day of March, in the year of our Lord eighteen hundred and sixty-three, shall be paid out of its own revenues.

8th. To promote the progress of science and useful arts, by securing, for limited times, to authors and inventors the exclusive right to their respective writings and discoveries.

9th. To constitute tribunals inferior to the Supreme Court.

10th. To define and punish piracies and felonies committed on the high seas, and offences against the law of nations.

11th. To declare war, grant letters of marque and reprisal, and make rules concerning captures on land and water.

12th. To raise and support armies; but no appropriations of money for that use shall be for a longer term than two years.

13th. To provide and maintain a navy.

14th. To make rules for government and regulation of the land and naval forces.

15th. To provide for calling forth the militia to execute the laws of the Confederate States, suppress insurrections, and repel invasions.

16th. To provide for organizing, arming, and disciplining the militia, and for governing such parts of them as may be employed in the service of the Confederate States, reserving to the States respectively the appointment of the officers and the authority of training the militia according to the discipline prescribed by Congress.

17th. To exercise exclusive legislation in all cases whatsoever over such district (not exceeding ten miles square) as may be by cession of one or more States and the acceptance of Congress become the seat of the Government of the Confederate States, and to exercise alike authority over all places purchased by the consent of the legislature of the State in which the same shall be for the erection of forts, magazines, arsenals, dockyards, and other needful buildings, and

18th. To make all laws which shall be necessary and proper for carrying into execution the foregoing powers, and all other powers vested by this constitution in the Government of the Confederate States, or in any department of office thereof.

§ 9. The importation of negroes of the African race from any foreign country, other than the slaveholding States or Territories of the United States of America, is hereby forbidden, and Congress is required to pass such laws as shall effectually prevent the same.

2d. Congress shall also have the power to prohibit the introduction of slaves from any State not a member of, or territory not belonging to, this Confederacy.

3d. The privilege of the writ of *habeas corpus* shall not be suspended, unless when in cases of rebellion or invasion the public safety may require it.

4th. No bill of attainder, or *ex post facto* law, or law denying or imparting the right of property in negro slaves, shall be passed.

5th. No capitation or other direct tax shall be laid unless in proportion to the census or enumeration herein before directed to be taken.

6th. No tax or duty shall be laid on articles exported from any State except by a vote of two-thirds of both Houses.

7th. No preference shall be given by any regulation of commerce or revenue to the ports of one State over those of another.

8th. No money shall be drawn from the treasury but in consequence of appropriations made by law, and a regular statement and account of the receipts and expenditures of all public money shall be published from time to time.

9th. Congress shall appropriate no money from the treasury except by a vote of two-thirds of both Houses—taken by yeas and nays, unless it be asked and estimated for by some one of the heads of departments and submitted to Congress by the President, or for the purpose of paying its own expenses and contingencies or for the payment of claims against the Confederate States, the justice of which shall have been judicially declared by a tribunal for the investigation of claims against the Government, which is hereby made the duty of Congress to establish.

10th. All bills appropriating money shall specify in federal currency the exact amount of each appropriation and the purpose for which it is made, and Congress shall grant no extra compensation to any public contractor, officer, agent, or servant, after such contract shall have been made or such service rendered.

11th. No title of nobility shall be granted by the Confederate States, and no person holding any office of profit or trust under them shall, without the consent of the Congress, accept of any present, emoluments, office, or title of any kind whatever, from any king, prince, or foreign State.

12th. Congress shall make no law respecting an establishment of religion or prohibiting the free exercise thereof, or abridging the freedom of speech, or of the press, or the right of the people peaceably to assemble and petition the Government for redress of grievances.

13th. A well regulated militia being necessary to the security of a free State, the right of the people to keep and bear arms shall not be infringed.

14th. No soldier shall in time of peace be quartered in any house without the consent of the owner, nor in time of war but in a manner prescribed by law.

15th. The right of the people to be secure in their persons, houses, papers, and against unreasonable searches and seizures, shall not be violated, and no warrant shall issue but upon probable cause, supported by oath or affirmation, and particularly describing the place to be searched and the person or things to be seized.

16th. No person shall be held to answer for a capital or otherwise infamous crime, unless on a presentment or indictment of a grand jury, except in cases arising in the land or naval forces or in the militia, when in actual service in time of war or public danger, nor shall any person be subject for the same offence to be twice put in jeopardy of life or limb, nor be compelled in any criminal case to be a witness against himself, nor be deprived of life, liberty, or property without due process of law, nor shall any private property be taken for public use without just compensation.

17th. In all criminal prosecutions the accused

shall enjoy the right to a speedy and public trial by an impartial jury of the State and district wherein the crime shall have been committed, which district shall have been previously ascertained by law, and to be informed of the nature and cause of the accusation, to be confronted with the witnesses against him, to have compulsory process for obtaining witnesses in his favor, and to have the assistance of counsel for his defence.

18th. In suits of common law where the value in controversy shall exceed twenty dollars, the right of trial by jury shall be preserved, and no fact so tried by a jury shall be otherwise re-examined in any court of the Confederacy than according to the rules of the common law.

19th. Excessive bail shall not be required, nor excessive fines imposed, nor cruel or unusual punishment inflicted.

20th. Every law or resolution having the force of law shall relate to but one subject, and that shall be expressed in the title.

§ 10. No State shall enter into any treaty, alliance or confederation, grant letters of marque and reprisals, coin money, make any thing but gold and silver coin a tender in payment of debts, pass any bill of attainder or *ex post facto* law, or law imparting the obligation of contracts, or grant any title of nobility.

2d. No State shall without the consent of Congress lay any imposts or duties on imports or exports except what may be absolutely necessary for executing its inspection law, and the net produce of all duties and imposts laid by any State on imports or exports shall be for the use of the Treasury of the Confederate States, and all such laws shall be subject to the revision and control of Congress.

3d. No State shall, without the consent of Congress lay any duty of tonnage except on sea-going vessels, for the improvement of its rivers and harbors navigated by the said vessels, but such duties shall not conflict with any treaties of the Confederate States with foreign nations, and any surplus of revenue thus derived shall after making such improvements be paid into the common Treasury, nor shall any State keep troops or ships of war in time of peace, enter into any agreement or compact with another State or with a foreign power to engage in war, unless actually invaded, or in such eminent danger as not to admit of delay. But when any river divides or flows through two or more States they may enter into compacts with each other to improve the navigation thereof.

ARTICLE II.

§ 1. The executive power shall be vested in a

President of the Confederate States of America. He and the Vice-President shall hold their offices for a term of six years, but the President shall not be re-eligible. The President and Vice-President shall be elected as follows:

2d. Each State shall appoint in such manner as the Legislature thereof may direct, a number of electors equal to the whole number of Senators and Representatives to which the State may be entitled in Congress, but no Senator or Representative, or person holding any office of trust or profit under the Confederate States shall be appointed an elector.

3d. The electors shall meet in their respective States and vote by ballot for President and Vice-President, one of whom at least, shall not be an inhabitant of the same State with themselves, they shall name in their ballots the person voted for as President, and in distinct ballots the person voted for as Vice-President, and they shall make distinct lists of all persons voted for as President, and of all persons voted for as Vice-President, and of the number of votes for each, which lists they shall sign and certify and transmit sealed to the Government of the Confederate States, directed to the President of the Senate. The President of the Senate shall, in presence of the Senate and House of Representatives, open all the certificates, and the votes shall then be counted, the person having the greatest number of votes for President shall be the President, if such number be a majority of the whole number of electors appointed, and if no person shall have such a majority, then from the persons having the highest numbers, not exceeding three on the list of those voted for as President, the House of Representatives shall choose immediately, by ballot, the President. But, in choosing the President, the votes shall be taken by States, the Representative from each State having one vote, a quorum for this purpose shall consist of a member or members from two-thirds of the States, and a majority of all the States shall be necessary to a choice. And if the House of Representatives shall not choose a President, whenever the right of choice shall devolve upon them, before the fourth day of March next following, then the Vice-President shall act as President, as in case of the death or other constitutional disability of the President.

4th. The person having the greatest number of votes as Vice-President shall be the Vice-President, if such number be a majority of the whole number of electors appointed, and if no person have a majority, then from the two highest numbers on the list, the Senate shall choose the Vice-President, a quorum for the purpose shall consist of two-thirds of the whole number of Senators, and a majority of the whole number shall be necessary for a choice.

5th. But no person constitutionally ineligible to the office of President, shall be eligible to that of Vice-President of the Confederate States.

6th. The Congress may determine the time of choosing the electors, and the day on which they shall give their votes, which day shall be the same throughout the Confederate States.

7th. No person except a natural born citizen of the Confederate States, or a citizen thereof at the time of the adoption of this Constitution, or a citizen thereof born in the United States, prior to the 20th December, 1860, shall be eligible to the office of President, neither shall any person be eligible to that office who shall not have attained the age of thirty-five years, and been fourteen years a resident within limits of the Confederate States, as they may exist at the time of his election.

8th. In case of the removal of the President from office, or of his death, resignation, or inability to discharge the powers and duties of the said office, the same shall devolve on the Vice-President, and the Congress may by law provide for the case of the removal, death, resignation or inability both of the President and the Vice-President, declaring what officer shall then act as President, and such officer shall then act accordingly until the disability be removed or a President shall be elected.

9th. The President shall, at stated times, receive for his services a compensation which shall neither be increased nor diminished during the period for which he shall have been elected, and he shall not receive within that period any other emolument from the Confederate States, or any of them.

10th. Before he enters on the execution of the duties of his office, he shall take the following oath or affirmation:

"I do solemnly swear (or affirm) that I will faithfully execute the office of President of the Confederate States and will, to the best of my ability preserve, protect, and defend the Constitution thereof.

§ 2. The President shall be commander-in-chief of the army and navy of the Confederate States, and of the militia of the several States when called into the actual service of the Confederate States. He may require the opinion in writing of the principal officer in each of the executive departments upon any subject relating to the duties of their respective offices, and he shall have the power to grant reprieves and pardons for offences against the Confederate States, except in cases of impeachment.

2d. He shall have power by and with the advice

and consent of the Senate to make treaties, provided two-thirds of the Senators present concur, and he shall nominate and, by and with the advice and consent of the Senate, shall appoint ambassadors, other public ministers and consuls, judges of the supreme court, and all other officers of the Confederate States whose appointments are not herein otherwise provided for and which shall be established by law; but the Congress may by law vest the appointment of such inferior officers as they think proper in the President alone, in the courts of law, or in the heads of departments.

3d. The principal officer in each of the executive departments, and all persons connected with the diplomatic service, may be removed at the pleasure of the President. All other civil officers of the executive department may be removed at any time by the President or other appointing power, when their services are unnecessary, or for dishonesty, incapacity, inefficiency, misconduct, or neglect of duty, and when so removed shall be reported to the Senate together with the reasons therefor.

4th. The President shall have power to fill all vacancies that may happen during the recess of the Senate by granting commissions, which shall expire at the end of the next session; but no person rejected by the Senate shall be reappointed to the same office during their ensuing recess.

§ 3. The President shall from time to time give to the Congress information of the state of the Confederacy, and recommend to their consideration such measures as he shall judge necessary and expedient; he may on extraordinary occasions convene both houses, or either of them, and in case of disagreement between them with respect to the time of adjournment, he may adjourn them to such time as he shall think proper; he shall receive ambassadors and other public ministers; he shall take care that the laws be faithfully executed, and shall commission all the officers of the Confederate States.

§ 4. The President and Vice-President, and all civil officers of the Confederate States, shall be removed on impeachment for, or conviction of, treason, bribery, or other high crimes and misdemeanors.

ARTICLE III.

§ 1. The judicial power of the Confederate States shall be vested in one superior court and in such inferior courts as the Congress may from time to time ordain and establish. The judges, both of the superior and inferior courts, shall hold their offices during good behavior, and shall at stated times receive for their services a compensation which shall not be diminished during continuance in office.

§ 2. The judicial power shall extend to all cases arising under the Constitution, the laws of the Confederate States, or treaties made or which shall be made under their authority, to all cases affecting ambassadors, other public ministers, and consuls, to all cases of admiralty, maritime jurisdiction, to controversies which the Confederate States shall be a party, to controversies between two or more States, between a State and citizens of another State where the State is plaintiff, between citizens claiming lands under grants of different States, and between a State or the citizens thereof and foreign States, citizens, or subjects; but no State shall be sued by a citizen or subject of any foreign State.

2d. In all cases affecting ambassadors, other public ministers and consuls, and those in which the State shall be a party, the supreme court shall have original jurisdiction. In all the other cases before mentioned the supreme court shall have appellate jurisdiction both as to law and fact, with such exceptions and under such regulations as the Congress shall make.

3d. The trial of all crimes, except in cases of impeachment, shall be by jury, and such trials shall be held in the State where the said crimes shall have been committed; but when not committed within any State, the trial shall be at such place or places as the Congress may by law have directed.

§ 3. Treason against the Confederate States shall consist only in levying a war against them, in adhering to their enemies, giving them aid and comfort. No person shall be convicted of treason unless on the testimony of two witnesses to the same, overt act, or on confession in open court.

2d. The Congress shall have power to declare the punishment of treason; but no attainder of treason shall work corruption of blood, or forfeiture, except during the life of the person attained.

ARTICLE IV.

§ 1. Full faith and credit shall be given in each State to the public acts, records, and judicial proceedings of every other State, and the Congress may by general laws prescribe the manner in which such acts, records, and proceedings shall be proved and the effect thereof.

§ 2. The citizens of each State shall be entitled to all the privileges and immunities of citizens of the several States, and shall have the right of transit and sojourn in any State of this Confederacy, with their slaves and other property; and the right of property in said slaves shall not be thereby impaired.

2d. A person charged in any State with treason, felony, or other crime against the laws of such State, who shall flee from justice and be found in another State, shall, on demand of the executive authority of the State from which he fled, be delivered up to be removed to the State having jurisdiction of the crime.

3d. No slave or other person held to service or labor in any State or Territory of the Confederate States under the laws thereof, escaping or unlawfully carried into another, shall, in consequence of any law or regulation therein, be discharged from such service or labor, but shall be delivered up on claim to the party to whom such slave belongs or to whom such service or labor may be due.

§ 3. Other States may be admitted into this Confederacy by a vote of two-thirds of the whole House of Representatives and two-thirds of the Senate—the Senate voting by States; but no new State shall be formed or erected within the jurisdiction of any other State, nor any State be formed by the junction of two or more States or parts of States without the consent of the legislators of the States concerned as well as of the Congress.

2d. The Còngress shall have power to dispose of and make all needful rules and regulations concerning the property of the Confederate States, including the lands thereof.

3d. The Confederate States may acquire new territory; and Congress shall have power to legislate and provide governments for the inhabitants of all territory belonging to the Confederate States, lying without the limits of the several States, and may permit them, at such times and in such manner as it may by law provide, to form States to be admitted into the Confederacy, in all such territory the institution of negro slavery as it now exists in the Confederate States shall be recognized and protected by Congress and the territorial government, and the inhabitants of the several Confederate States and territories shall have the right to take to such territory any slaves lawfully held by them in any of the States or territories of the Confederate States.

4th. The Confederate States shall guarantee to every State that now is or hereafter may become a member of this Confederacy a republican form of government, and shall protect each of them against invasion, and on application of the legislature (or of the executive when the legislature is not in session) against domestic violence.

ARTICLE V.

§ 1. Upon the demand of any three States, legally assembled in their several conventions, the Congress shall summon a convention of all the States to take into consideration such amendments to the constitution as the said States shall concur in suggesting at the time when the said demand is made, and should any of the proposed amendments to the constitution be agreed on by the said convention, voting by the States, and the same be ratified by the legislatures of two-thirds of the several States, or by conventions of two-thirds thereof—as the one or the other mode of ratification may be proposed by the general convention—they shall thenceforward form a part of this constitution; but no State shall without its consent be deprived of its equal representation in the Senate.

ARTICLE VI.

§ 1. The government established by this constitution is the successor of the provisional government of the Confederate States of America, all the laws passed by the latter shall continue in force until the same shall be repealed or modified, and all the officers appointed by the same shall remain in office until their successors are appointed and qualified, or the offices abolished.

2d. All debts contracted and engagements entered into before the adoption of this constitution shall be as valid against the Confederate States under this constitution as under the provisonal government.

3d. This constitution and the laws of the Confederate States may, in persuance thereof, and all treaties made or which shall be made under the authority of the Confederate States, shall be the supreme law of the land, and the judges in every State shall be bound therein, by any thing in the constitution or laws of any State to the contrary notwithstanding.

4th. The senators and representatives before mentioned, and the members of the several State legislatures, and all executive and judicial officers, both of the Confederate States and of the several States, shall be bound by oath or affirmation to support this constitution; but no religious test shall ever be required as qualification to any office of public trust under the Confederate States.

5th. The enumeration in the constitution of certain rights, shall not be construed to deny or disparage others retained by the people of the several States.

6th. The powers not delegated to the Confederate States by the constitution, nor prohibited by it to the States, are reserved to the States respectively, or to the people thereof.

ARTICLE VII.

§ 1. The ratification of the convention of five

States shall be sufficient for the establishment of this constitution between the States so ratifying the same.

When five States shall have ratified this constitution in a manner before specified, the Congress under the provisional constitution shall prescribe the time for holding the election for President and Vice-President, and for the meeting of the electoral college, and for counting the votes, and for inaugurating the President. They shall also prescribe the time for holding the first election of members of Congress under this constitution, and the time for assembling the same.

Until the assembling of such Congress, the Congress under the provisional constitution shall continue to exercise the legislative powers granted them, not extending beyond the time limited by the Constitution of the provisional government.

Adopted unanimously, March 11, 1861.

THE CONFEDERATE CABINET AND CONGRESS.

President—JEFFERSON DAVIS, of Mississippi.
Vice-President—ALEX. H. STEPHENS, of Georgia.
Secretary of State—JUDAH P. BENJAMIN, of La.
Secretary of War—JAMES A. SEDDON, of Va.
Sec. of Treasury—CHAS. G. MEMMINGER, of S. C.
Sec. of Navy—STEPHEN R. MALLORY, of Florida.
Attorney-General—THOMAS H. WATTS, of Ala.
Postmaster-General—JAMES H. REAGAN, of Texas.

FIRST REGULAR CONGRESS—SENATE.

Congress met at Richmond, on the 2d Monday in Jan., 1863.

A. H. STEPHENS, of Georgia, *President.*
R. M. T. HUNTER, of Virginia, *President pro tem.*

ALABAMA.
Clement C. Clay
William L. Yancey.

ARKANSAS.
Robert W. Johnson
Charles B. Mitchell.

FLORIDA.
James M. Baker
Augustus E. Maxwell.

GEORGIA.
Benjamin H. Hill
Herschel V. Johnson.

KENTUCKY.
Henry C. Burnett
William E. Simms.

LOUISIANA.
Thos. J. Semmes
Edward Sparrow.

MISSISSIPPI.
Albert G. Brown
James Phelan.

MISSOURI.
John B. Clark
Robert S. T. Peyton.

NORTH CAROLINA.

George Davis
William T. Diortch.

SOUTH CAROLINA.

Robert W. Barnwell
James L. Orr.

TENNESSEE.

Landon C. Haynes
Gustavus A. Henry.

TEXAS.

Wm. S. Oldham
Lewis T. Wigfall.

VIRGINIA.

Robert M. T. Hunter
Allen T. Caperton.

HOUSE OF REPRESENTATIVES.

THOMAS S. BOCOCK, of Virginia, *Speaker.*

ALABAMA.

1 Thomas J. Foster,
2 William R. Smith,
3 John P. Ralls,
4 Jabez L. McCurry,
5 Francis S. Lyon,
6 William P. Chilton,
7 David Clopton,
8 James L. Pugh,
9 Edward L. Dargan,

ARKANSAS.

1 Felly I. Batson,
2 Grand D. Royston,
3 A. H. Garland,
4 Thomas B. Henley.

FLORIDA.

1 James B. Dawkins,
2 Robert B. Hilton.

GEORGIA.

1 Julian Hartridge,
2 C. J. Munnerlyn,
3 Hines Holt,
4 Augustus H. Kenan,
5 David W. Lewis,
6 William W. Clark,
7 Robert P. Trippe,
8 Lucius J. Gartrell,
9 Hardy Strickland,
0 Augustus R. Wright.

KENTUCKY.

1 Alfred Boyd,
2 John W. Crockett,
3 H. E. Reid,
4 George W. Ewing,
5 James S. Christman,
6 T. L. Burnett,
7 H. W. Bruce,
8 S. S. Scott,
9 E. M. Bruce,
10 J. W. Moore,
11 R. J. Breckinridge,
12 John M. Elliott.

LOUISIANA.

1 Charles J. Viders,
2 Charles M. Conrad,
3 Duncan F. Kenner,
4 Lucien J. DuPre,
5 John F. Lewis,
6 John Perkins, jr.

MISSISSIPPI.

1 J. W. Clapp,
2 Reuben Davis,
3 Israel Welsh,
4 H. C. Chambers,
5 O. R. Singleton,
6 E. Barksdale,
7 John J. McRae.

MISSOURI.

1 W. M. Cooke,
2 Thomas A. Harris,
3 A. H. Conrow,
4 Casper W. Bell,
5 George G. Vest,
6 T. W. Freeman,
7 John Hyer.

NORTH CAROLINA.

1 Wm. H. N. Smith,
2 Robert R. Bridgers,
3 Owen R. Keenan,
4 T. D. M. Dowell,
5 Thomas S. Ashe,
6 A. H. Arlington,
7 Robert Lander,
8 William Lander,
9 Burgess S. Gaither,
10 A. T. Davidson.

SOUTH CAROLINA.

1 John McQueen,
2 W. Porcher Miles,
3 L. M. Ayer,
4 Milledge L. Bonham,
5 James Farrow,
6 W. W. Boyce.

TENNESSEE.

1 Joseph T. Heiskell,
2 William G. Swan,
3 W. B. Tobbs,
4 E. L. Gardenshire,
5 Henry S. Foote,
6 Meredith P. Gentry,
7 George W. Jones,
8 Thomas Meneese,
9 J. D. C. Atkins,
10 John V. Wright,
11 David M. Currin.

TEXAS.

1 John A. Wilcox,
2 C. C. Herbert,
3 Peter W. Gray,
4 B. F. Sexton,
5 M. D. Graham,
6 W. B. Vaughn.

VIRGINIA.

1 M. R. H. Garnett,
2 John R. Chambliss,
3 James Lyons,
4 Roger A. Pryor,
5 Thomas S. Bocock,
6 John Goode, jr,
7 J. P. Hencombe,
8 D. C. De Jarnette,
9 William Smith,
10 A. R. Boteler,
11 John R. Baldwin,
12 Waller R. Staples,
13 Walter Preston,
14 Samuel A. Miller,
15 Robert Johnston,
16 Charles W. Russell.

INAUGURAL ADDRESS OF JEFFERSON DAVIS.

Gentlemen of the Congress of the Confederate States of America, Friends and Fellow-Citizens:

Called to the difficult and responsible station of Chief Executive of the Provisional Government which you have instituted, I approach the discharge of the duties assigned me with an humble distrust of my abilities, but with a sustaining confidence in the wisdom of those who are to guide and aid me in the administration of public affairs, and an abiding faith in the virtue and patriotism of the people. Looking forward to the speedy establishment of a permanent government to take the place of this, and which by its greater moral and physical power will be better able to combat with the many difficulties which arise from the conflicting interests of separate nations, I enter upon the duties of the office to which I have been chosen, with the hope that the beginning of our career as a confederacy may not be obstructed by hostile opposition to our enjoyment of the separate existence and independence which we have asserted, and which, with the blessing of Providence, we intend to maintain.

Our present condition, achieved in a manner unprecedented in the history of nations, illustrates the American idea that governments rest upon the consent of the governed, and that it is the right of the people to alter and abolish governments whenever they become destructive to the ends for which they were established. The declared compact of the Union from which we have withdrawn was to establish justice, ensure domestic tranquillity, provide for the common defence, promote the general welfare, and secure the blessings of liberty to ourselves and our posterity; and when in the judgment of the sovereign States now composing this Confederacy, it has been perverted from the purposes for which it was ordained, and ceased to answer the ends for which it was established, a peaceful appeal to the ballot-box declared that, so far as they were concerned, the government created by that compact should cease to exist. In this they merely asserted the right which the Declaration of Independence of 1776 defined to be inalienable. Of the time and occasion of its exercise they as sovereigns were the final judges, each for itself. The impartial, enlightened verdict of mankind will vindicate the rectitude of our conduct; and He who knows the hearts of men will judge of the sincerity with which we labored to preserve the government of our fathers in in its spirit.

The right solemnly proclaimed at the birth of the States, and which has been affirmed and reaffirmed in the bills of rights of the States subsequently admitted into the Union of 1789, undeniably recognizes in the people the power to resume the authority delegated for the purposes of government. Thus the sovereign States here represented, proceeded to form this Confederacy; and it is by the abuse of language that their act has been denominated revolution. They formed a new alliance, but within each State its government has remained. The rights of person and property have not been disturbed. The agent through whom they communicated with foreign nations is changed, but this does not necessarily interrupt their international relations. Sustained by the consciousness that the transition from the former Union to the present Confederacy has not proceeded from a disregard on our part of our just obligations or any failure to perform every constitutional duty, moved by no interest or passion to invade the rights of others, anxious to cultivate peace and commerce with all nations, if we may not hope to avoid war, we may at least expect that posterity will acquit us of having needlessly engaged in it. Doubly justified by the absence of wrong on our part, and by wanton aggression on the part of others, there can be no cause to doubt the courage and patriotism of the people of the Confederate States will be found equal to any measures of defence which soon their security may require.

An agricultural people, whose chief interest is the export of a commodity required in every manufacturing country, our true policy is peace, and the freest trade which our necessities will permit. It is alike our interest and that of all those to whom we would sell and from whom we would buy, that there should be the fewest practicable restrictions upon the interchange of commodities. There can be but little rivalry between ours and any manufacturing or navigating community, such as the northeastern States of the American Union. It must follow, therefore, that mutual interest would invite good will and kind offices. If, however, passion or lust of dominion should cloud the judgment or inflame the ambition of those States, we must prepare to meet the emergency and maintain by the final arbitrament of the sword the position which we have assumed among the nations of the earth.

We have entered upon a career of independence, and it must be inflexibly pursued through many years of controversy with our late associates of the Northern States. We have vainly endeavored to secure tranquillity and obtain respect for the rights to which we were entitled. As a necessity, not a choice, we have resorted to the remedy of separation, and henceforth our energies must be directed to the conduct of our own affairs, and the perpetuity of the confederacy which we have formed. If a just perception of mutual interest shall permit us peaceably to pursue our separate political career, my most earnest desire will have been fulfilled. But if this be denied us, and the integrity of our territory and jurisdiction be assailed, it will but remain for us with firm resolve to appeal to arms and invoke the blessing of Providence on a just cause.

As a consequence of our new condition, and with a view to meet anticipated wants, it will be necessary to provide a speedy and efficient organization of the branches of the Executive department having special charge of foreign intercourse, finance, military affairs, and postal service. For purposes of defence the Confederate States may, under ordinary circumstances, rely mainly upon their militia; but it is deemed advisable in the present condition of affairs, that there should be a well instructed, disciplined army, more numerous than would usually be required on a peace establishment. I also suggest that, for the protection of our harbors and commerce on the high seas, a navy adapted to those objects will be required. These necessities have, doubtless, engaged the attention of Congress.

With a Constitution differing only from that of our fathers in so far as it is explanatory of their well known intent, freed from sectional conflicts, which have interfered with the pursuit of the general welfare, it is not unreasonable to expect that the States from which we have recently parted may seek to unite their fortunes to ours, under the govenment which we have instituted. For this your Constitution makes adequate provision, but beyond this, if I mistake not, the judgment and will of the people are, that union with the States from which they have separated is neither practicable nor desirable. To increase the power, develop the resources, and promote the happiness of the Confederacy, it is requisite there should be so much homogeneity that the welfare of every portion would be the aim of the whole. Where this does not exist antagonisms are engendered which must and should result in separation.

Actuated solely by a desire to preserve our own rights, and to promote our own welfare, the separation of the Confederate States has been marked by no aggression upon others, and followed by no domestic convulsion. Our industrial pursuits have received no check, the cultivation of our fields progresses as heretofore, and even should we be involved in war there would be no considerable diminution in the production of the staples which have constituted our exports, in which the commercial world has an interest scarcely less than our own. This common interest of producer and consumer can only be intercepted by an exterior force which should obstruct its transmission to foreign markets, a course of conduct which would be detrimental to manufacturing and commercial interests abroad.

Should reason guide the action of the government from which we have separated, a policy so detrimental to the civilized world, the Northern States included, could not be dictated by even a stronger desire to inflict injury upon us; but if it be otherwise, a terrible responsibility will rest upon it, and the suffering of millions will bear testimony to the folly and wickedness of our aggressors. In the meantime there will remain to us, besides the ordinary remedies before suggested, the well known resources for retaliation upon the commerce of an enemy.

Experience in public stations of a subordinate

grade to this which your kindness has conferred, has taught me that care and toil and disappointments are the price of official elevation. You will see many errors to forgive, many deficiencies to tolerate; but you shall not find in me either want of zeal or fidelity to the cause that is to me the highest in hope and of most enduring affection. Your generosity has bestowed upon me an undeserved distinction, one which I neither sought nor desired. Upon the continuance of that sentiment, and upon your wisdom and patriotism, I rely to direct and support me in the performance of the duties required at my hands.

We have changed the constituent parts but not the system of our government. The Constitution formed by our fathers is that of these Confederate States. In their exposition of it, and in the judicial construction it has received, we have a light which reveals its true meaning. Thus instructed as to the just interpretation of that instrument, and ever remembering that all offices are but trusts held for the people, and that delegated powers are to be strictly construed, I will hope by due diligence in the performance of my duties, though I may disappoint your expectation, yet to retain, when retiring, something of the good will and confidence which will welcome my entrance into office.

It is joyous in the midst of perilous times to look around upon a people united in heart, when one purpose of high resolve animates and actuates the whole, where the sacrifices to be made are not weighed in the balance, against honor, right, liberty, and equality. Obstacles may retard, but they cannot long prevent the progress of a movement sanctioned by its justice and sustained by a virtuous people. Reverently let us invoke the God of our fathers to guide and protect us in our efforts to perpetuate the principles which by his blessing they were able to vindicate, establish, and transmit to their posterity; and with a continuance of His favor ever gratefully acknowledged, we may hopefully look forward to success, to peace, to prosperity.

SPEECH OF PRESIDENT DAVIS,

AT RICHMOND, JUNE 1ST, 1861.

FRIENDS AND FELLOW-CITIZENS: I thank you for the compliment your presence conveys. It is an indication of regard, not for the person, but for the position which he holds. The cause in which we are engaged is the cause of the advocacy of rights to which we were born, those for which our fathers of the Revolution bled—the richest inheritance that ever fell to man, and which it is our sacred duty to transmit to our children.

Upon us is devolved the high and holy responsibility of preserving the constitutional liberty of a free government. Those with whom we have lately associated have shown themselves so incapable of appreciating the blessings of the glorious institutions they inherited, that they are to-day stripped of the liberty to which they were born. They have allowed an ignorant usurper to trample upon all the prerogatives of citizenship, and to exercise powers never delegated to him; and it has been reserved to your own State, so lately one of the original thirteen, but, now, thank God, fully separated from them, to become the theatre of a great central camp, from which will pour forth thousands of brave hearts to roll back the tide of this despotism.

Apart from that gratification we may well feel at being separated from such a connection, is the pride that upon you devolves the task of maintaining and defending our new Government. I believe that we shall be able to achieve this noble work, and that the institutions of our fathers will go to our children as safely as they have descended to us.

In these Confederate States we observe those relations which have been poetically ascribed to the United States, but which never there had the same reality—States so distinct that each existed as a Sovereign, yet so united that each was wound with the other to constitute a whole; or, as more beautifully expressed, "Distinct as the billows, yet one as the sea."

Upon every hill which now overlooks Richmond you have had, and will continue to have, camps containing soldiers from every State in the Confederacy; and to its remotest limits every proud heart beats high with indignation at the thought that the foot of the invader has been set upon the soil of old Virginia. There is not one true son of the South who is not ready to shoulder his musket, to bleed, to die, or to conquer in the cause of liberty here.

Beginning under many embarrassments, the result of seventy years taxation being in the hands of our enemies, we must at first move cautiously. It may be that we shall have to encounter sacrifices; but, my friends, under the smiles of the God of the Just, and filled with the same spirit that animated our fathers, success shall perch on our banners. I am sure you do not expect me to go into any argument upon those questions which, for twenty-five years, have agitated the country. We have now reached the points where, arguments being exhausted, it only remains for us to stand by our weapons.

When the time and occasion serve, we shall smite the smiter with manly arms, as did our fathers before us, and as becomes their sons. To the enemy we leave the base acts of the assassin and incendiary, to them we leave it to insult helpless women; to us belongs vengeance upon man.

Now, my friends, I thank you again for this gratifying manifestation. (A voice. "Tell us some thing of Buena Vista.")

Well, my friends, I can only say we will make the battle fields in Virginia another Buena Vista, and drench with blood more precious than that which flowed there. We will make a history for ourselves. We do not ask that the past shall shed our lustre upon us, bright as our past has been, for we can achieve our own destiny.

We may point to many a field, over which has floated the flag of our country when we were of the United States—upon which Southern soldiers and Southern officers reflected their brave spirits in their deeds of daring; and without intending to cast a shadow upon the courage of any portion of the United States, let me call it to your remembrance, that no man who went from these Confederate States has ever yet, as a general officer, surrendered to an enemy.

Pardon me if I do not go into matters of history, and permit me, again, to thank you for this kind manifestation of your regard, to express to you my hearty wishes for the individual prosperity of you all, with the hope that you will all pray to God to crown our cause and our country with success.

He then retired from the windows amid prolonged cheers.

Calls were then made for ex-Governor Wise, to which, after a short delay, he responded as follows:

SPEECH OF EX-GOVERNOR HENRY A. WISE.

My Friends: You all know that I am a civil soldier only, and that in that capacity I was nearly worn down in the siege of the Virginia Convention. Thank God, however, that with a little rest, some help, and some damage, from the doctors, I have been enabled to recruit my exhausted energies.

The time of deliberation has given place to the time of action, and I have taken up my bed as an individual, in common with others, to march to Richmond to meet the President of our now separate and independent republic. I am ready to obey his orders, not only with pride, pleasure, and devotion to the cause, and respect to the office he fills, but with respect to the man himself as one who has our fullest confidence.

You have to meet a foe with whom you could not live in peace. Your political powers and rights. which were enthroned in that Capitol when you were united with them under the old constitutional bond of the Confederacy, have been annihilated. They have undertaken to annul laws within your own limits that would render your property unsafe within those limits. They have abolitionized your border, as the disgraced North-west will show. They have invaded your moral strongholds and the rights of your religion, and have undertaken to teach you what should be the moral duties of men.

They have invaded the sanctity of your homes and firesides, and endeavored to play master, father, and husband for you in your households ; in a word, they would set themselves up as a petty Providencee by which you are in all things to be guided and controlled. But you have always declared that you would not be subject to this invasion of your rights.

Though war was demanded, it was not for you to declare war. But now that the armies of the invader are hovering around the tomb of Washington, where is the Virginian heart that does not beat with a quicker pulsation at this last and boldest desecration of his beloved State? Their hordes are already approaching our metropolis, and extending their folds around our State as does the anaconda around his victim. The call is for action.

I rejoice in this war. Who is there that now dares to put on sanctity to depreciate war, or the "horrid glories of war." None. Why? Because it is a war of purification. You want war, fire, blood, to purify you; and the Lord of Hosts has demanded that you should walk through fire and blood. You are called to the fiery baptism, and I call upon you to come up to the altar. Though your pathway be through fire, or through a river of blood, turn not aside. Be in no hurry—no hurry and flurry.

Collect yourselves, summon yourselves, elevate yourselves to the high and sacred duty of patriotism. The man who dares to pray, the man who dares to wait until some magic arm is put into his hand; the man who will not go unless he have a Minié, or percussion musket, who will not be content with flint and steel, or even a gun without a lock, is worse than a coward—he is a renegade. If he can do no better, go to a blacksmith, take a gun along as a sample, and get him to make you one like it. Get a spear—a lance. Take a lesson from John Brown. Manufacture your blades from old iron, even though it be the tires of your cart-wheels. Get a bit of carriage spring, and grind and burnish it in the shape of a bowie knife, and put it to any sort of a handle, so that it be strong—ash, hickory, oak. But, if possible, get a double-barrelled gun and a dozen rounds of buckshot, and go upon the battle-field with these.

If their guns reach further than yours, reduce the distance; meet them foot to foot, eye to eye, body to body, and when you strike a blow, strike home. Your true-blooded Yankee will never stand still in the face of cold steel. Let your aim, therefore, be to get into close quarters, and with a few decided, vigorous movements, always pushing forward, never back, my word for it, the soil of Virginia will be swept of the Vandals who are now polluting its atmosphere.

The band then struck up "Dixie," which was followed by "We may be Happy yet."

PROCLAMATION BY JEFFERSON DAVIS,

GRANTING LETTERS OF MARQUE.

Whereas, ABRAHAM LINCOLN, the President of the United States, has, by proclamation, announced the intention of invading this Confederacy with an armed force, for the purpose of capturing its fortresses, and thereby subverting its independence, and subjecting the free people thereof to the dominion of a foreign power; and whereas it has thus become the duty of this Government to repel the threatened invasion, and to defend the rights and liberties of the people by all the means which the laws of nations and the usages of civilized warfare place at its disposal;

Now, therefore, I, JEFFERSON DAVIS, *President of the Confederate States of America*, do issue this my Proclamation, inviting all those who may desire, by service in private armed vessels on the high seas, to aid this Government in resisting so wanton and wicked an aggression, to make application for commissions or Letters of Marque and Reprisal, to be issued under the seal of these Confederate States.

And I do further notify all persons applying for Letters of Marque, to make a statement in writing, giving the name and a suitable description of the character, tonnage, and force of the vessel, and the name and place of residence of each owner concerned therein, and the intended number of the crew, and to sign said statement and deliver the same to the Secretary of State, or to the Collector of any port of entry of these Confederate States, to be by him transmitted to the Secretary of State.

And I do further notify all applicants aforesaid that before any commission or Letter of Marque is issued to any vessel, the owner or owners thereof, and the commander for the time being, will be required to give bonds to the Confederate States, with at least two responsible sureties, not interested in such vessel, in the penal sum of five thousand dollars; or if such vessel be provided with more than one hundred and fifty men, then in the penal sum of ten thousand dollars, with condition that the owners, officers and crew who shall be employed on board such commissioned vessels shall observe the laws of these Confederate States and the instructions given to them for the regulation of their conduct. That they shall satisfy all damages done contrary to the tenor thereof by such vessel during her commission, and deliver up the same when revoked by the President of the Confederate States.

And I do further specially enjoin on all persons holding offices, civil and military, under the authority of the Confederate States, that they be vigilant and zealous in discharging the duties incident thereto; and I do, moreover, solemnly exhort the good people of these Confederate States, as they love their country, as they prize the blessings of free government, as they feel the wrongs of the past and these now threatened in aggravated form by those whose enmity is more implacable because unprovoked, that they exert themselves in preserving order, in promoting concord, in maintaining the authority and efficacy of the laws, and in supporting and invigorating all the measures which may be adopted for the common defence, and by which, under the blessings of Divine Providence, we may hope for a speedy, just, and honorable peace.

In testimony whereof, I have hereunto set my hand, and caused the seal of the Confederate States to be affixed, this *seventeenth* day of April, 1861.

By the President,

(Signed) JEFFERSON DAVIS.

R. TOOMBS, Secretary of State.

SPEECH OF HON. A. H. STEPHENS,

AT ATLANTA, GA., APRIL 30, 1861.

MY FELLOW-CITIZENS:—I think the country may be considered safe, since your interest in its welfare has brought you out at this hour of the night. I have just returned from a mission to old Virginia. It will be gratifying to you, I know, to state that she is not only out of the Union, but *she is a member of the Southern Confederacy, and has sent delegates to our Congress, now assembled.* North Carolina will have her delegates with us, also, in a few days. Her Legislature meets to-morrow, and I doubt not *she will be out of the Union before Saturday night.* The fires which first kindled the old Mecklenburgh Declaration of Independence are again burning throughout all her domains. From all that we have learned in the last few days, Tennessee will soon put herself on the side of the South, and be a new star in our shining galaxy. The news is also good from

Kentucky, though I have nothing official from there. A few of her public men are trying to put the brakes down on her people; but they seem unwilling to submit any longer. From Missouri the news is most cheering, and Arkansas will soon be with us.

But the best of all is, that Maryland—gallant little Maryland—right under the guns of Lincoln and the threats of Blair, to make it a Free State, if the blood of the last white man has to be shed in accomplishing it—*has resolved, to a man, to stand by the South!* She will be arrayed against Abolitiondom, and cling to the South; and if she has not delegates with us now, she is in open defiance of Lincoln and his Government, and will soon be with us, even by revolution. The cause of Baltimore is the cause of us all, from the Atlantic to the Rio Grande. Her hands must be held up, and triumph must be assured to her.

You have probably seen it stated that overtures of peace had been made by Lord Lyons, and, perhaps, by other parties. I tell you it is not true, and is only intended to deceive you. It is also said that the Lincoln Government has done so. This may be true; but if it is, it is all for treachery, as they gave traitorous assurances to our Commissioners at Washington. For weeks they were kept there under the most positive assurances of a pacific policy and intentions towards us—all with the basest motives that can actuate a treacherous heart. If peace propositions are made by them now, I conjure you not to trust them for a single moment—they only intend to deceive and betray—to lull your energies and suspicions, till they secure some cowardly advantage.

Our enemies say that they only want to protect the public property; and yet I have it from unquestioned authority that they have mined all the public buildings in Washington—the Capitol and all the other Departments—for the purpose of destroying them. They have called out 75,000 men, they say to protect the public property now in their possession, and to retake and protect that which they have been forced to give up; yet, wherever they are now, they have prepared to destroy the property, and have destroyed, or attempted to destroy, all that we have compelled them to relinquish, because of their intentions to use it for the purpose of subjugating us. Sumter was mined to be blown up on leaving it. Much of the property was burned up at Harper's Ferry, in hastily vacating that place; and an attempt was made to burn up not only all the public property on leaving Gosport Navy Yard, but the whole city of Norfolk. This is one of the most remarkable instances on record where Providence was on our side. Plans were laid to burn up the Navy Yard and the whole city. The incendiary fires were lighted; and, if their intentions had succeeded, such a conflagration had never been witnessed on this continent, and would have been second only to the burning of Moscow; but, just at the critical moment, before the ravages had extended, the wind turned! The winds of Heaven turned, and stayed the spread of the devouring element. The same wind that kind Heaven sent to keep off the fleet at Charleston till Sumter was reduced, came to the relief of Norfolk at the critical moment. Providence was signally on our side. They attempted to blow up the Dock, the most expensive one on the continent—but there was a break in the train they had laid, and it failed. They attempted to burn down the old *Pennsylvania*, *Germantown*, and the *Merrimac*. They set the match, while they endeavored to get out of the way of their intended destruction; but the vessels sunk before the fire caught—another remarkable instance of the interposition of Providence on our behalf, and the strongest evidence of our rectitude. We were right at first, are right now, and shall keep ourselves right to the end.

What is to take place before the end I know not. A threatening war is upon us, made by those who have no regard for right! We fight for our homes, our fathers and mothers, our wives, brothers, sisters, sons, and daughters, and neighbors! *They for* MONEY! The hirelings and mercenaries of the North are all hand to hand against you.

As I told you when I addressed you a few days ago, Lincoln may bring his seventy-five thousand soldiers against us; but seven times seventy-five thousand men can never conquer us. We have now Maryland and Virginia, and all the Border States with us. We have ten millions of people with us, heart and hand, to defend us to the death. *We can call out a million of people, if need be; and when they are cut down, we can call out another, and still another*, until the last man of the South finds a bloody grave, rather than submit to their foul dictation. But a triumphant victory and independence, with an unparalled career of glory, prosperity and progress awaits us in the future. *God is on our side, and who shall be against us?* None but His omnipotent hand can defeat us in this struggle.

A general opinion prevails that Washington city is soon to be attacked. On this subject I can only say, our object is peace. We wish no aggressions on any one's rights, and will make none. But *if Maryland secedes*, the District of Columbia will fall to her by reversionary right—the same as Sumter to South Carolina, Pulaski to Georgia, and Pickens to

Alabama. When we have the right we will demand the surrender of Washington, just as we did in the other cases, and will enforce our demands at every hazard and at whatever cost. And here let me say that our policy and conduct from the first have been right, and shall be to the last. I glory in this consciousness of our rectitude.

It may be that "whom the gods would destroy, they first make mad." But for Lincoln's wicked and foolish war proclamation, the border States—some of them at least, would still have lingered in the hope that the Administration and its designs were not so basely treacherous as that document has shown them to be. Tennessee and other States would have lingered for some time. Now, all the slave States are casting in their lot with us, and linking their destinies with ours. We might afford to thank Lincoln a little for showing his hand. It may be that soon the Confederate flag with fifteen stars will be hoisted upon the dome of the ancient Capitol. If so, God's will be done, is my prayer. Let us do nothing that is wrong. Let us commit our cause into His hand—perform our whole duty, and trust in Him for the crowning results.

I have many things I would like to say to you, but my strength will not admit, even if it were necessary for your encouragement—but it is not. I find that you are fully up to the music, that you thoroughly comprehend our condition, and are resolved to do your whole duty. I find our people everywhere are alive to their interests and their duty in this crisis. Such a degree of popular enthusiasm was never before seen in this country. I find my fellow-citizens all along the railroad line eager to hear the news, and to speed our glorious cause with their services. This is the fifth speech which I have made since I left home this evening at 5 o'clock. In my town, yesterday, a meeting was held, a company was organized, and their services tendered to our government. A flag was made in two hours by our patriotic ladies and presented to the company, and $2,200 was raised to equip the company and take care of the needy families of soldiers who may go off to fight for their country.

My friends, *forget not the soldier!* Send him contributions to make him comfortable while he is in the service. Take care of his family while he is absent. Employ your hands and your substance in doing works of charity in this day of your country's trial. If any should fall in the battle, remember the orphan and the widow, and take care of them. God will bless you in the noble performances of a patriotic duty.

My fellow-citizens, I must close these remarks.

I am gratified to meet you to-night. I am gratified that Georgia and all the South is a unit. I rejoice to be able to tell you the welcome news that Virginia is a unit. Nearly every single member of her Convention will sign the Ordinance of Secession. And now, with my best wishes, I bid you good-night.

His speech was rapturously applauded throughout; and, as he retired, three cheers for Stephens were given with a will.

In a few moments, in response to earnest solicitations, he again came on the platform, and said:

The news from Washington is very interesting. It has been stated in the newspapers—first, that the Virginia troops had occupied Arlington Heights, just across the Potomac from the President's house; and again, that Lincoln's troops had occupied that point. My information is that both these statements are incorrect. Lincoln, however, has occupied Georgetown Heights. He has from fifteen to twenty thousand soldiers stationed in and about Washington. Troops are quartered in the Capitol, who are defacing its walls and ornaments with grease and filth, like a set of vandal hordes. The new Senate chamber has been converted into a kitchen and quarters—cooking and sleeping apparatus have actually been erected and placed in that elegant apartment.

The Patent Office is converted into soldiers' barracks, and is ruined with their filth. The Post-Office Department is made a storehouse for barrels of flour and bacon. All the departments are appropriated to base uses, and despoiled of their beauty by those treacherous, destructive enemies of our country. Their filthy spoliations of the public buildings, and works of art at the Capital, and their preparations to destroy them, are strong evidence to my mind that they do not intend to hold or defend the place; but to abandon it, after having despoiled and laid it in ruins. Let them destroy it—savage-like—if they will. We will rebuild it. Phœnix-like, new and more substantial structures will rise from its ashes. Planted anew, under the auspices of our superior institutions, it will live and flourish throughout all ages.

SPEECH OF J. M. MASON.

AT RICHMOND, VA., JUNE 8, 1861.

Soldiers of the Maryland Line: I am deputed to do a most grateful duty; first, in the name of Virginia, to give you an earnest and cordial welcome to the "Old Dominion;" and next, to present to you, in behalf of the ladies of Maryland, this flag. I see, soldiers of Maryland, that you are "rough and ready"—the highest honor of a soldier in revolutionary times. We all know who you are. We all know what brought you here, and we are all ready, as I trust you have experienced, to extend to you a soldier's welcome—the only welcome, indeed, that can be extended in times like these. Your own honored State is with us heart and soul in this great controversy. By your enterprise, your bravery, and your determined will, you have escaped from the thraldom of tyranny which envelopes that State; and you know, I know—for I have been among its people—we all know, that the same spirit which brought you here, actuates thousands who remain at home. (Applause.) I welcome you, soldiers of Maryland, upon the threshold of the second great war of independence—a war that will be transmitted by history to the future as the greatest of two wars of independence; a war that is waged against the South with less provocation, less reason, less regard to humanity and honor, than was that waged by the mother country in 1776.

Your presence here is proof that you participate in this sentiment. And I tell you further, my countrymen, in view of these circumstances, there is not a man among you who will dare to return to Maryland with that flag dishonored. Not one. I tell you further, there is not a man among you who will dare to return to Maryland except as a soldier in victory. Do you ask me why? Because we are engaged in a great and holy war of self-defence. In after ages, when history records the transactions of this epoch—when the passions of men shall have subsided, and the historian can take a calm and philosophical view of the events which have led to the present collision between the two sections, he will write that the people of the Southern States understood and protected civil liberty, and that the misguided North either did not comprehend, or abandoned it? For what have we witnessed? The spectacle of the Chief Justice of the United States, the man who stands at the head of the principal department of the Federal Government—the man who has illustrated in his life, for more than four generations, all that adorns honor, virtue, and patriotism—a native-born citizen of your own State of Maryland—Roger B. Taney—that man has put the judicial fiat of condemnation upon the Government of the United States for its shameless abandonment of the very corner stone of our liberties. A native Marylander, he remains at home to defend the last refuge of civil liberty against the atrocious aggressions of a remorseless tyranny. I honor him for it; the world will honor him, posterity will honor him; and there will be inscribed upon his monument the highest tribute ever paid to a man. He has stood bravely in the breach, and interposed the unspotted arm of justice between the rights of the South and the malignant usurpation of power by the North. There he still remains, "a cloud by day and a pillar of fire by night," to direct the welfare of our nation in this atrocious aggression upon our liberty.

Now, my countrymen, why are you here? What has brought you across the border? What is your mission to Virginia? You tell your own tale.

You have arms in your hands; you are under a gallant leader, and you are to march under a flag honored by the ladies of your own State, worked by their own fair hands. You are here not merely to fight our battles. No, I am not so selfish as to presume that; but to fight the battles of civil liberty in behalf of the entire South. You are on a high mission.

You are not the first Marylanders who have crossed the border. We had, in the days of the first Revolution, a Maryland line, whose name has passed into history without one blot upon its fair escutcheon – a Maryland line who illustrated upon every field in the South their devotion to the civil liberty of that day—a Maryland line, who, in the remote savannahs of the Carolinas, spilled their blood like water at Camden, at Guilford Court House, at the Cowpens, and at Eutaw, where the last battle was fought, and the enemy finally surrendered. They were your ancestry. They travelled barefooted, unclothed, without blankets or tents, and but few muskets, and you came after them. But you have this peculiar distinction: You are volunteers in a double sense—you are volunteers for the war, and you are volunteers for the great cause of the South against the aggressions of the North. You are no strangers; you are our neighbors. My own home is upon the confines of your State. I went there, four weeks ago, immediately after Virginia had denounced the unholy movements in the North, to learn the spirit of your people. I went to Fredericktown, where the Legislature were assembled, anxious to ascertain whether Virginia could rely upon you in the hour of trial. I knew the political incubus by which your people were crushed to the earth; but such were the indications I perceived on every side, that when I returned to Virginia I unhesitatingly reported that Maryland is with the South. I staked my word upon it as a man of principle and a man of truth. The giant arm of the oppressor has been too strong for the time being, but the spirit is still alive, unsubdued and unrepressed. You are here to confirm this fact by your presence.

You are in Richmond. What is Richmond? It is a large city—a city of gallant men and refined women; a city whose inhabitants are engaged in all the useful and honorable pursuits of life tending to the advance of civilization and prosperity. At the present moment, however, Richmond is a huge camp, where but one mind, one heart, and one determination animates every occupant, man, woman, and child. (Applause.) Our wives, mothers—and I appeal to the ladies, if I may not also say our sweethearts—have entered into it with a zest, which shows that their hearts and affections are fully in the work. You will have no child's play. There is no time now for vain boasting. I confide as much as I can in the prowess of the men of this section, and you will be false to the fame of your fathers if you are not victors; but your enemies relies upon mere brute force. There are doubtless brave soldiers among them whom it will be hard to conquer, but you will remember that you are fighting for your fathers, mothers, and firesides. They are mercenaries fighting for pay, you are men fighting for your homes and rights. All you require is subsistence. "Give us," you say, "the means of living, the arms to fight with, and show us the enemy." (Applause.) It may be, that in the providences of war, not one among all those who are before me will return. You may come here, if necessary, to lay your lives upon the altar of your country, and I feel assured that every man will do his duty.

I will tell you an incident connected with the Alabama troops. They were attended by a minister of the Gospel, who was a guest at my house. He told me that he had with him a purse of gold, which had been given to him by the parents of two young men in the ranks, with injunction that it should be sacredly preserved during the war, unless his sons should fall upon the field of battle. Then, said the father, " Give them a Christian burial." There was a patriot father, who had devoted his sons to the service of his country, and that man does not stand alone.

Such is the object with which you have engaged in this war. The true duty of the soldier is not merely to fight a battle or kill an enemy. He has also to endure the trials of the camp ; the weariness of the forced march ; the vigilance of day and night ; the restraints of discipline, and the patience to bear with discomforts and disappointments. This is the real test of courage, and he who comes out of the war with the reputation of having thus done his duty through the sunshine and through storm, is the true man, and the thorough soldier.

But I will not detain you longer, except to dis charge the grateful duty which remains, of presenting to you, in behalf of the ladies of Baltimore, this beautiful banner. There it is unfurled before you for the first time. There are emblazoned the fifteen stars of the Southern States, looking prospectively to the day when they will all be with us ! The star of Maryland is among them, and the women of your State have put it there, confiding it to your safe keeping. Look upon it as a sacred trust. In passing through the storm of battle, it may be tattered and soiled, but I believe I can say that you will bring it back without a spot of dishonor upon it. But you are not only to return that flag here—you are to take it back to Baltimore. (Cheers, and cries of "We will.") It came here in the hands of the fair lady who stands by my side, who brought it through the camp of the enemy, with a woman's fortitude, courage, and devotion to our cause; and you are to take it back to Baltimore, unfurl it in your streets, and challenge the applause of your citizens. (Applause.)

SAM HOUSTON'S SPEECH,

AT INDEPENDENCE, TEXAS, MAY 10.

THE troubles which have come upon the community are neither unexpected to me, nor do I fail to realize all the terrible consequences yet to ensue. Since the passage of the Nebraska and Kansas bill, I have had but little hope of the stability of our institutions. The advantages gained to the North by that measure, through the incentive to Anti-Slavery agitation and the opening of a vast territory to Free-Soil settlement, were such that I saw that the South would soon be overslaughed, and deprived of equality in the Government—a state of things which a chivalrous people like ours would not submit to. Yet I fostered the longing hope that when the North saw the dangers of disunion, and beheld the resolute spirit with which our people met the issue, they would abandon their aggressive policy, and allow the Government to be preserved and administered in the same spirit with which our forefathers created it. For this reason I was conservative. So long as there was a hope of obtaining our rights, and maintaining our institutions, through an appeal to the sense and justice and the brotherhood of the Northern people, I was for preserving the Union. The voice of hope was weeks since drowned by the guns of Fort Sumter. It is not now heard above the tramp of invading armies. The mission of the Union has ceased to be one of peace and equality, and now the dire alternative of yielding tamely before hostile armies, or meeting the shock like freemen, is presented to the South. Sectional prejudices, sectional hate, sectional aggrandizement, and sectional pride, cloaked in the name of the Government and Union, stimulate the North in prosecuting this war. Thousands are duped into its support by zeal for the Union, and reverence for its past associations; but the motives of the Administration are too plain to be misunderstood.

The time has come when a man's section is his country. I stand by mine. All my hopes, my fortunes, are centred in the South, When I see the land for whose defence my blood has been spilt, and the people whose fortunes have been mine through a quarter of a century of toil, threatened with invasion, I can but cast my lot with theirs and await the issue.

For years I have been denounced on account of my efforts to save the South from the consequences of the unhappy measures which have brought destruction upon the whole country. When, in the face of almost my entire section, and a powerful Northern strength, I opposed the Kansas and Nebraska bill, the bitterness of language was exhausted to decry and villify me. When I pictured the consequences of that measure, and foretold its effects, I was unheeded. Now, when every Northern man who supported that measure is demanding the subjugation of the South, our people can see the real feelings which actuate them in supporting it. Devoted as I was to peace and to the Union, I have struggled against the realization even of my own prophecies. Every result I foresaw has already occurred. It was to bring peace and strength to the South. It has brought war, and spread free soil almost to the northern border of Texas. All we can now do is to stand firm by what we have, and be more wise in the future.

The trouble is upon us; and no matter how it came, or who brought it on, we have to meet it. Whether we have opposed this secession movement or favored it, we must alike meet the consequences. I sought calm and prudent action. I desired a united and prepared South, if we must leave the

Union. Entire coöperation may not now be possible, but we have ample strength for the struggle if we husband it aright. We must fight now whether we are prepared or not.

My position was taken months since. Though I opposed secession for the reasons mentioned, I saw that the policy of coercion could not be permitted. The attempt to stigmatize and crush out this revolution, comprehending States and millions of people, as a rebellion, would show that the Administration at Washington did not comprehend the vast issues involved, or refused to listen to the dictates of reason, justice, and humanity. A stubborn resort to force when moderation was necessary, would destroy every hope of peace and the reconstruction of the Union. That my views on this point might not be misunderstood, I sent to the Legislature, prior to the passage of the Secession Ordinance by the Convention, a message, in which I said:

"Having called you together to provide for an expression of the sovereign will of the people at the ballot box, I also deem it my duty to declare that, while the people of the State of Texas are deliberating upon this question, no impending threats of coercion from the people of another State should be permitted to hang over them, without at least the condemnation of their representatives. Whatever that sovereign will may be when fairly expressed, it must be maintained. Texas, as a man, will defend it. While the executive would not counsel foolish bravado, he deems it a duty we owe to the people, to declare that, even though their action shall bring upon us the consequences which now seem impending, we shall all (be our views in the past and present what they may) be united."

Now that not only coercion, but a vindictive war is about to be inaugurated, I stand ready to redeem my pledge to the people. Whether the Convention acted right or wrong is not now the question. Whether I was treated justly or unjustly is not now to be considered. I put all that under my feet, and there it shall stay. Let those who have stood by me do the same, and let us show that at a time when peril environs our beloved land, we know how to be patriots and Texans.

Let us have no past, except the glorious past, whose heroic deeds shall stimulate us to resistance to oppression and wrong, and burying in the grave of oblivion all our past difficulties, let us go forward, determined not to yield from the position which the people have assumed until our independence is acknowledged, or if not acknowledged, wrung from our enemies by the force of our valor. It is no time to turn back now—the people have put their hands to the plow; they must go forward. To recede would be worse than ignominy. Better meet war in its deadliest shape than cringe before an enemy whose wrath we have invoked. I make no pretensions as to myself. I have yielded up office and sought retirement to preserve peace among our people. My services, perhaps, are not important enough to be desired. Others are perhaps more competent to lead the people through this revolution. I have been with them through the fiery ordeal once, and I know that with prudence and discipline their courage will surmount all obstacles. Should the tocsin of war, calling forth the people to resist the invader, reach the retirement to which I shall go, I will heed neither the denunciations of my enemies, nor the charms of my own fireside, but will join the ranks of my countrymen to defend Texas once again. Then I will ask those who have pursued me with malignity, and who have denounced me as a traitor to Texas and the South, to prove themselves more true, when the battle shock shall come. Old and worn as I am, I shall not be laggard. Though others may lead, I shall not scorn to follow; and though I may end life in the ranks, where I commenced it, I shall feel that the post of duty is the post of honor.

We have entered upon a conflict which will

demand all the energies of the people. Not only must they be united, but all the heroic virtues which characterize a free people must be brought into requisition. There must be that sacrificing spirit of patriotism which will yield the private desires for the public good. There must be that fortitude which will anticipate occasional reverses as the natural consequences of war, and meet them with becoming pride and resignation; but, above all, there must be discipline and subordination to law and order. Without this, armies will be raised in vain, and carnage will be wasted in hopeless enterprises. The South, chivalric, brave, and impetuous as it is, must add to these attributes of success thorough discipline, or disaster will come upon the country. The Northern people by their nature and occupation are subordinate to orders. They are capable of great endurance and a high state of discipline. A good motto for a soldier is, Never underrate the strength of your enemy. The South claims superiority over them in point of fearless courage. Equal them in point of discipline, and there will be no danger. Organize your forces; yield obedience to orders from headquarters. Do not waste your energies in unauthorized expeditions; but in all things conform to law and order, and it will be ten times better than running hither and thither, spending money and time, without accomplishing any of the plans of a campaign which your leaders have marked out. Once organized, stay organized.

Do not be making companies to-day and unmaking them to-morrow. If you are dissatisfied with your captain, wait until the battle day comes, and he gets killed off, then you can get another. It is better to fight up to him and get rid of him in that way than to split off, and make a new company to be split up in the same way. I give this advice as an old soldier. I know the value of subordination and discipline. A good citizen, who has been obedient to law and civil authority, always makes a good soldier. I have ever been conservative, was conservative as long as the Union lasted—am a conservative citizen of the Southern Confederacy, and giving to the constituted authorities of the country, civil and military, and the Government which a majority of the people have approved and acquiesced in, an honest obedience, I feel that I should do less than my duty did I not press upon others the importance of regarding this the first duty of a good citizen.

SPEECH OF HOWELL COBB,

AT ATLANTA, GEORGIA, MAY 22.

Fellow-Citizens: I feel that I cannot compensate you for the trouble you have taken to call me out. You, as citizens of Atlanta, know that there has been no instance of my being called upon by you, in which I failed to respond, unless for the very good reason that I had *nothing to say;* and this evening I must offer this excuse for failing to address you at length. I presume that a curiosity to know what we have been doing in the Congress recently assembled at Montgomery, has induced you to make this call upon me.

We have made all the necessary arrangements to meet the present crisis. Last night we adjourned to meet in Richmond on the 20th of July. I will tell you why we did this. The "Old Dominion," as you know, has at last shaken off the bonds of Lincoln, and joined her noble Southern sisters. Her soil is to be the battle ground, and her streams are to be dyed with Southern blood. We felt that her cause was our cause, and that if she fell we wanted to die with her. (Cheers.) We have sent our soldiers on to the posts of danger, and we wanted to be there to aid and counsel our brave "boys." In the progress of the war, further legislation may be necessary, and we will be there, that when the hour of danger comes, we may lay aside the robes of legislation, buckle on the armor of the soldier, and do battle beside the brave ones who have volunteered for the defence of our beloved South. (Loud cheers.)

The people are coming up gallantly to the work. When the call was made for twelve months' volunteers, thousands were offered; but when it was changed to the full term of the war, *the numbers increased!* The anxiety among our citizens is not as to who shall *go* to the wars, but *who shall stay at home?* No man in the whole Confederate States—the gray haired sire down to the beardless youth—in whose veins was one drop of Southern blood, feared to plant his foot upon Virginia's soil, and die fighting for our rights.

In Congress, the other day, I told them that if no other arm was raised to defend Virginia, noble old Georgia—proud in her love of independence—would rise up to a man, and crossing to the southernmost bound of Abolitionism, would say to Lincoln and his myrmidons, "Thus far, *traitor!* shalt thou come; but *no farther!*" (Tremendous applause.) This good old commonwealth—solitary and alone, if need be—will fight until she sees the last foul invader in his grave! And I know, fellow-citizens, that there is no loyal son of Georgia before me, whose heart does not beat a warm response to this pledge. (Cries of, "We will! we will!")

But we not only need soldiers, we must have treasure to carry on this war. Private contributions have been offered to a vast amount. I will mention an instance which occurred on the Mississippi a few days ago. An aged man—whose gray hairs and tottering limbs forbade his entering the ranks, and whose children of the first and second generations were in the ranks of his country's defenders—was asked how much he would give to carry on the war. The spirit of the old man rose up in him—"Tell them," he said, "that my yearly crop of 1,000 bales of cotton they may have. Only give me enough to sustain me, and let the balance go to my country!" Offers of this sort come pouring in upon the Government from all parts of the country.

But the Government does not require contributions from individuals; she has the means within herself of sustaining this war. No donations are necessary, except for the equipment of your own volunteers and those you can and will provide for. But I tell you what you may do. Those of you who raise large crops of cotton, when your cotton is ready for market, give it to your Government at its market value, receive in return its bonds, and let it sell your produce to Europe for the specie to sustain our brave "boys" in Virginia. This was agreed on at Montgomery, and we promised to throw out the suggestion, that the people might think about it.

I raise some cotton, and every thing above my necessary expenses my Government shall have. When this was proposed in Congress, a gentleman from Mississippi rose up and said that he did not raise cotton; it was his misfortune not to be able to help his country in that manner. "But," said he, "I will go home and canvass my section, and every man that I meet, who raises cotton, sugar, and rice, I will persuade him to sell it to his Government."

But this patriotism is not confined to the men; the women, with warm hearts and busy fingers, are helping the soldiers. I will give you an instance that happened at Montgomery. A message was received on Friday evening that a thousand sand bags were wanted, with which to build batteries to protect our men at Pensacola. What could be done? Some one suggested that the ladies be made acquainted with our wants. It was Saturday morning. Monday evening I received a notice to attend a meeting to be held at 5 o'clock in the Methodist church. Between the reception of the message and 5 o'clock that evening, the money had been raised, the cloth purchased, and the lovely women of that city, with their own delicate hands, at their homes and in the sanctuary of the living God, were making bags; and on Tuesday I saw the sand bags start for Pensacola, to protect our brave soldiers! (Cheers.) Talk about *subjugating* us! Why, we might lay aside the men, and all Abolitiondom *couldn't run down the women even!* (Prolonged applause.)

They say at the North that we are alarmed. What cause have we to be so? When the Congress assembled at Montgomery there were only six States represented. Now there are nine, and every breeze that comes from Tennessee bears us news that her people are rising up unanimously against the usurpations of Lincoln. North Carolina—the State of my parentage, and I love her with a love next to my native State—she, too, is aroused, and her Convention has unanimously adopted the ordinance of secession; and these States will soon shine as bright stars in our galaxy. With such aids as these, and with so many brave hearts in our land, we can *never be conquered!*

I have spoken enthusiastically, but pardon me. I can say nothing more. (Cries of, "Go on!") You will excuse me, as I have been speaking at every town on the road, and am quite hoarse.

GEN. R. E. LEE'S ADDRESS TO HIS TROOPS.

HEADQUARTERS ARMY NORTHERN VIRGINIA,
October 2d, 1862.

IN reviewing the achievements of the army during the present campaign, the commanding general cannot withhold the expression of his admiration of the indomitable courage it has displayed in battle, and its cheerful endurance of privation and hardship on the march.

Since your great victories around Richmond yon have defeated the enemy at Cedar Mountain, expelled him from the Rappahannock, and, after a conflict of three days, utterly repulsed him on the plains of Manassas, and forced him to take shelter within the fortifications around his capital.

Without halting for repose, you crossed the Potomac, stormed the heights of Harper's Ferry made prisoners of more that 11,000 men, and captured upwards of seventy pieces of artillery, all their small arms, and other munitions of war.

While one corps of the army was thus engaged, the other ensured its success by arresting at Boonsboro' the combined armies of the enemy, advancing under their favorite general to the relief of their beleaguered comrades.

On the field of Sharpsburg, with less than one-third his numbers, you resisted, from daylight until dark, the whole army of the enemy, and repulsed every attack along his entire front of more than four miles in extent.

The whole of the following day you stood prepared to resume the conflict on the same ground, and retired next morning, without molestation, across the Potomac. Two attempts, subsequently made by the enemy, to follow you across the river, have resulted in his complete discomfiture and being driven back with loss.

Achievements such as these demand much valor and patriotism. History records few examples of greater fortitude and endurance than this army has exhibited; and I am commissioned by the President to thank you in the name of the Confederate States for the undying fame you have won for their arms.

Much as you have done, much more remains to be accomplished. The enemy again threaten us with invasion, and to your tried valor and patriotism the country looks with confidence for deliverance and safety. Your past exploits give assurance that this confidence is not misplaced.

R. E. Lee,
Commanding General.

SPEECH OF HON. A. H. STEPHENS.

AT RICHMOND, VA., APRIL 22, 1861.

THE distinguished gentleman was introduced to the throng by Mayor Mayo, and received with hearty cheers. In response, Mr. Stephens returned his acknowledgments for the warmth of the personal greeting, and his most profound thanks for it as the representative of the Confederate States. He spoke of the rejoicing the secession of Virginia had caused among her Southern sisters. Her people would feel justified if they could hear it as he had. North Carolina was out, and did not know exactly how she got out. The fires that were blazing here he had seen all along his track from Montgomery to Richmond. At Wilmington he had counted on the street twenty flags of the Confederate States.

The news from Tennessee was equally cheering—there the mountains were on fire. Some of the States still hesitated, but soon all would be in.

Tennessee was no longer in the late Union. She was out by the resolutions of her popular assemblies in Memphis and other cities. Kentucky would soon be out; her people were moving. Missouri—who could doubt the stand she would take?—when her Governor, in reply to Lincoln's insolent proclamation, had said: "You shall have no troops for the furtherance of your illegal, unchristian, and diabolical schemes!" Missouri will soon add another star to the Southern galaxy. Where Maryland is you all know. The first Southern blood has been shed on her soil, and Virginia would never stand by and see her citizens shot down. The cause of Baltimore is the cause of the whole South.

He said the cause we were engaged in was that which attached people to the Constitution of the late United States—it was the cause of civil, religious, and constitutional liberty. Many of us looked at the Constitution as the anchor of safety. In Georgia the people had been attached to the previous Union, but the Constitution which governed it was framed by the Southern talent and understanding. Assaults had been made on it ever since it was established.

Lately a latitudinous construction had been made by the North, while we of the South sought to interpret it as it was—advocating strict construction,

State rights, the right of the people to rule, &c. He spoke of all the fifteen Southern States as advocating this construction. To violate the principles of the Constitution was to initiate revolution; and the Northern States had done this.

The Constitution framed at Montgomery discarded the obsolete ideas of the old Constitution, but had preserved its better portion, with some modifications, suggested by the experience of the past; and it had been adopted by the Confederate States, who would stand by it. The old Constitution had been made an engine of power to crush out liberty; that of the Confederate States to preserve it. The old Constitution was improved in our hands, and those living under it had, like the phœnix, risen from their ashes.

The revolution lately begun did not effect alone property, but liberty. He alluded to Lincoln's call for 75,000 volunteers, and said he could find no authority in the old Constitution for such a flagrant abuse of power. His second proclamation had stigmatized as pirates all who sailed in letters of marque; this was also in violation of the Constitution, which alone gave Congress that power.

What had the friends of liberty to hope for? Beginning in usurpation, where would it end? You are, however, said he, no longer under the rule of this tyrant. With strong arms and stout hearts you have now resolved to stand in the defence of liberty. The Confederate States have but asserted their rights. They believed that their rulers derived their just powers from the consent of the governed. No one had the right to deny the existence of the sovereign right of secession. Our people did not want to meddle with the Northern States—only wanted the latter to leave them alone. When did Virginia ever ask the assistance of the General Government?

If there is sin in our institutions, we bear the blame, and will stand acquitted by natural law, and the higher law of the Creator. We stand upon the law of God and Nature. The Southern States did not wish to resort to arms after secession. Mr. Stephens alluded to the negotiations between Major Anderson and the authorities of the Confederate States, to demonstrate the proposition. History, he said, if rightly written, will acquit us of a desire to shed our brother's blood.

The law of necessity and of right compelled us to act as we did. He had reason to believe that the Creator smiled on it. The Federal flag was taken down without the loss of a single life. He believed that Providence would be with us and bless us to the end. We had appealed to the God of Battles for the justness of our cause. Madness and folly ruled at Washington. Had it not have been so, several of the States would have been in the Union for a year to come. Maryland would join us, and may be, ere long, the principles that Washington fought for might be again administered in the city that bore his name.

Every son of the South, from the Potomac to the Rio Grande, should rally to the support of Maryland. If Lincoln quits Washington as ignominiously as he entered it, God's will will have been accomplished. The argument was now exhausted. Be prepared; stand to your arms—defend your wives and firesides. He alluded to the momentous consequences of the issue involved. Rather than be conquered, let every second man rally to drive back the invader. The conflict may be terrible, but the victory will be ours. Virginians, said he, you fight for the preservation of your sacred rights—the land of Patrick Henry—to keep from desecration the tomb of Washington, the graves of Madison, Jefferson, and all you hold most dear.

THE LAST MANIFESTO OF THE CONFEDERATE CONGRESS.

JUNE 15, 1864.

Joint resolution declaring the dispositions, principles and purposes of the Confederate States in relation to the existing war with the United States.

Whereas, It is due to the great cause of humanity and civilization, and especially to the heroic sacrifices of their gallant army in the field, that no means, consistent with a proper self-respect, and the approved usages of nations, should be omitted by the Confederate States to enlighten the public opinion of the world with regard to the true character of the srruggle in which they are engaged, and the dispositions, principles and purposes by which they are actuated; therefore,

Resolved by the Congress of the Confederate States of America, That the following manifesto be issued in their name and by their authority, and that the President be requested to cause copies thereof to bs transmitted to our commissioners abroad, to the end that the same may be laid before foreign Governments.

MANIFESTO OF THE CONGRESS OF CONFEDERATE STATES OF AMERICA, RELATIVE TO THE EXISTING WAR WITH THE UNITED STATES.

The Congress of the Confederate States of America, acknowledging their responsibility to the opinion of the civilized world, to the great law of Christian philanthropy, and to the Supreme Ruler of the universe, for the part they have been compelled to bear in this sad spectacle of war and carnage which this continent has, for the last three years, exhibited to the eyes of afflicted humanity, deems the present a fitting occasion to declare the principles, the sentiments and the purposes by which they have been and are still actuated.

They have ever deeply deplored the necessity which constrained them to take up arms in defence of their rights and of the free institutions derived from their ancestors; and there is nothing they more ardently desire than peace, whensoever their enemy, by ceasing from the unhallowed war waged upon them, shall permit them to enjoy in peace the sheltering protection of those hereditary rights and of those cherished institutions. The series of successes with which it has pleased Almighty God, in so signal a manner, to bless our arms on almost every point of our invaded border since the opening of the present campaign, enables us to profess this desire of peace, in the interests of civilization and humanity, without danger of having our motives misinterpreted, or of the declaration being ascribed to any unmanly sentiment, or any distrust of our ability fully to maintain our cause. The repeated and disastrous checks, foreshadowing ultimate discomfiture, which their gigantic army, directed against the capital of the Confederacy, has already met with, are but a continuation of the same providential successes for us. We do not refer to these successes in any spirit of vain boasting, but in humble acknowledgment of that Almighty protection which has vouchsafed and granted them.

The world must now see that eight millions of people, inhabiting so extensive a territory, with such varied resources and such numerous facilities for defence as the benignant bounty of nature has bestowed upon us, and animated with one spirit to encounter every privation and sacrifice of ease, of health, of property, of life itself, rather than be degraded from the condition of free and independent States into which they were born, can never be conquered. Will not our adversaries themselves begin to feel that humanity has bled long enough; that tears and blood and treasure enough have been expended in a bootless undertaking, covering their own land, no less than ours, with a pall of mourning, and exposing them, far more than ourselves, to the catastrophe of financial exhaustion and bankruptcy, not to speak of the loss of their liberties by the despotism engendered in an aggressive warfare upon the liberties of another and kindred people? Will they be willing, by a longer perseverance in a wanton and hopeless contest, to make this continent, which they so long boasted to be the chosen abode of liberty and self-government, of peace and a higher civilization, the theatre of the most causeless and prodigal effusion of blood which the world has ever seen, of a virtual relapse into the barbarism of the ruder ages, and of the destruction of constitutional freedom by the lawlessness of usurped power?

These are questions which our adversaries will decide for themselves. We desire to stand acquitted before the tribunal of the world, as well as in the eyes of omniscient justice, of any responsibility for the origin or prolongation of a war as contrary to the spirit of the age as to the traditions and acknowledged maxims of the political system of America.

On this continent, whatever opinions may have

prevailed elsewhere, it has ever been held and acknowledged by all parties that government, to be lawful, must be founded on the consent of the governed. We were forced to dissolve our federal connection with our former associates by their aggressions on the fundamental principles of our compact of union with them; and in doing so, we exercised a right consecrated in the great charter of American liberty—the right of a free people, when a government proves destructive of the ends for which it was established, to recur to original principles and to institute new guards for their security. The separate independence of the States, as sovereign and co-equal members of the Federal Union, had never been surrendered; and the pretension of applying to independent communities, so constituted and organized, the ordinary rules for coercing and reducing rebellious subjects to obedience, was a solecism in terms, as well as an outrage on the principles of public law.

The war made upon the Confederate States was, therefore, wholly one of aggression. On our side, it has been strictly defensive. Born freemen, and the descendants of a gallant ancestry, we had no option but to stand up in defence of our invaded firesides, of our desecrated altars, of our violated liberties and birthright, and of the prescriptive institutions which guard and protect them. We have not interfered, nor do we wish, in any manner whatever, to interfere with the internal peace and prosperity of the States arrayed in hostility against us, or with the freest development of their destinies in any form of action or line of policy they may think proper to adopt for themselves. All we ask, is a like immunity for ourselves, and to be left in the undisturbed enjoyment of those inalienable rights of "life, liberty and the pursuit of happiness," which our common ancestors declared to be the equal heritage of all the parties to the social compact.

Let them forbear aggressions upon us, and the war is at an end. If there be questions which require adjustment by negotiation, we have ever been willing and are still willing to enter into communication with our adversaries in a spirit of peace, of equity, and manly frankness. Strong in the persuasion of the justice of our cause, in the gallant devotion of our citizen-soldiers, and of the whole body of our people, and above all in the gracious protection of Heaven, we are not afraid to avow a sincere desire for peace, on terms consistent with our honor and the permanent security of our rights, and an earnest aspiration to see the world once more restored to the benificent pursuits of industry and of mutual intercourse and exchanges, so essential to its well-being, and which have been so gravely interrupted by the existence of this unnatural war in America.

But if our adversaries, or those whom they have placed in authority, deaf to the voice of reason and justice, settled against the dictates of both prudence and humanity by a presumptuous and delusive confidence in their own numbers, or those of their black and foreign mercenaries, shall determine upon an indefinite prolongation of the contest, upon them be the responsibility of a decision so ruinous to themselves and so injurious to the interests and repose of mankind.

For ourselves, we have no fear of the result. The wildest picture ever drawn of a disordered imagination comes short of the extravagance which could dream of the conquest of eight millions of people, resolved with one mind "to die freemen rather than live slaves," and forewarned by the savage and exterminating spirit in which this war has been waged upon them, and by the mad avowals of its patrons and supporters, of the worse than Egyptian bondage that awaits them in the event of their subjugation.

With these declarations of our dispositions, our principles, and our purposes, we commit our cause to the enlightened judgment of the world, to the sober reflections of our adversaries themselves, and to the solemn and righteous arbitrament of Heaven.

THE LAST PROCLAMATION OF PRESIDENT DAVIS.

DANVILLE, VA., April 5, 1865.

THE General-in-Chief found it necessary to make such movements of his troops as to uncover the capital. It would be unwise to conceal the moral and material injury to our cause resulting from the occupation of our capital by the enemy. It is equally unwise and unworthy of us to allow our own energies to falter, and our efforts to become relaxed under reverses, however calamitous they may be. For many months the largest and finest army of the Confederacy, under a leader whose presence inspires equal confidence in the troops and the people, has been greatly trammelled by the necessity of keeping constant watch over the approaches to the capital, and has thus been forced to forego more than one opportunity for promising enterprise. It is for us, my countrymen, to show by our bearing under reverses how wretched has been the self-deception of those who have believed us less able to endure misfortune with fortitude than to encounter dangers with courage.

We have now entered upon a new phase of the struggle. Relieved from the necessity of guarding particular points, our army will be free to move from point to point, to strike the enemy in detail far from his base. Let us but will it, and we are free.

Animated by that confidence in your spirit and fortitude which never yet failed me, I announce to you, fellow-countrymen, that it is my purpose to maintain your cause with my whole heart and soul; that I will never consent to abandon to the enemy one foot of the soil of any of the States of the Confederacy. That Virginia—noble State—whose ancient renown has been eclipsed by her still more glorious recent history; whose bosom has been bared to receive the main shock of this war; whose sons and daughters have exhibited heroism so sublime as to render her illustrious in all time to come—that Virginia, with the help of the people, and by the blessing of Providence, *shall be held and defended*, and no peace ever be made with the infamous invaders of her territory.

If by the stress of numbers we should ever be

compelled to a temporary withdrawal from her limits, or those of any other Border State, we will return until the baffled and exhausted enemy shall abandon in despair his endless and impossible task of making slaves of a people resolved to be free.

Let us, then, not despond, my countrymen, but, relying on God, meet the foe with fresh defiance, and with unconquered and unconquerable hearts.

JEFFERSON DAVIS.

GENERALS OF THE CONFEDERATE ARMY.*

GENERALS.

1. Samuel Cooper, Virginia, adjutant general.
2. Albert S. Johnston, Texas, commanding in Kentucky.
3. Joseph E. Johnston, Virginia, commanding Northern Virginia.
4. Robert E. Lee, Virginia, commanding South Atlantic coast.
5. P. G. T. Beauregard, Louisiana, commanding Army of Potomac.
6. Braxton Bragg, Louisiana, commanding at Pensacola.

* This list refers generally to the first period of the war. There were, of course, many shiftings of command, promotions, changes in the names of military departments, &c., that it is impossible to include. The early Confederate armies in Virginia were known as "the Army of the Potomac" and "the Army of the Shenandoah." Afterwards there were only known two great army organizations in the Confederacy, east of the Mississippi River—"the Army of Northern Virginia" and "the Army of Tennessee."

LIEUTENANT-GENERALS.

1. Leonidas Polk, Louisiana, commanding at Memphis.

2. Earl Van Dorn, Mississippi, Army of Potomac.

3. Theophilus H. Holmes, North Carolina, Army of Potomac.

4. James Longstreet, Alabama, Army of Potomac.

5. Thomas J. Jackson, Virginia, commanding Northwestern Virginia.

6. Edmund Kirby Smith, Florida, Army of Potomac.

7. Richard S. Ewell, Virginia, Army of Potomac.

MAJOR-GENERALS.

1. David E. Twiggs, Georgia, resigned.

2. Gustavus W. Smith, Kentucky, Army of Potomac.

3. William J. Hardee, Georgia, Missouri.

4. Benjamin Huger, South Carolina, commanding at Norfolk.

5. John B. Magruder, Virginia, commanding at Yorktown.

6. Mansfield Lovell, Virginia, commanding coast of Louisiana.

7. George. B. Crittenden, Kentucky, commanding East Tennessee.

8. Milledge L. Bonham, South Carolina, Army of Potomac.

9. John B. Floyd, Virginia, commanding Army of Kanawha.

10. Henry A. Wise, Virginia, waiting orders.

11. Ben McCulloch, Texas, Missouri.

12. Henry R. Jackson, Georgia, resigned.

13. Robert S. Garnett, Virginia, killed in action.

14. William H. T. Hill, Georgia, resigned.

15. Bernard E. Bee, South Carolina, killed in action.

16. Alexander R. Lawton, Georgia, commanding coast of Georgia.

17. Gideon J. Pillow, Tennessee, Kentucky.

18. Samuel R. Anderson, Tennessee, Kentucky.

19. Daniel S. Donelson, Tennessee, coast of South Carolina.

20. David R. Jones, South Carolina, Army of Potomac.

21. Jones M. Withers, Alabama, commanding coast of Alabama.

22. John C. Pemberton, Virginia, coast of South Carolina.

23. John H. Winder, Maryland, Richmond.

24. Jubal A. Early, Virginia, Army of Potomac.

25. Thomas B. Flournoy, Arkansas, died in Arkansas.

26. Samuel Jones, Virginia, Army of Potomac.

27. Arnold Elzey, Maryland, Army of Potomac.

28. Daniel H. Hill, North Carolina, Army of Potomac.

29. Henry H. Sigley, Louisiana, Texas frontier.

30. William H. C. Whiting, Georgia, Army of Potomac.

31. William H. Loring, North Carolina, Western Virginia.

32. Richard H. Anderson, South Carolina, Pensacola.

33. Albert Pike, Arkansas, Indian Commissioner.

34. Thomas T. Fauntleroy, Virginia, resigned.

35. Robert Toombs, Georgia, Army of Potomac.

36. Daniel Ruggles, Virginia, Louisiana.

37. Charles Clark, Mississippi, Army of Potomac.

38. Roswell S. Ripley, South Carolina, coast of South Carolina.

39. Isaac R. Trimble, Maryland, Army of Potomac.

40. John B. Grayson, Kentucky, died in Florida.

41. Paul O. Hebert, Louisiana, coast of Texas.

42. Richard C. Catlin, North Carolina, commanding coast of North Carolina.

43. Felix K. Zollicoffer, Tennessee, Eastern Kentucky.

44. Benj. F. Cheatham, Tennessee, Kentucky.

45. Joseph R. Anderson, Virginia, coast of North Carolina.

46. Simon B. Buckner, Kentucky, Kentucky.

47. Leroy Pope Walker, Alabama, Alabama.

48. Albert G. Blanchard, Louisiana, Norfolk.

49. Gabriel S. Rains, North Carolina, Yorktown.

50. J. E. B. Stuart, Virginia, Army of Potomac.

51. Lafayette McLaws, Georgia, Yorktown.

52. Thomas F. Drayton, South Carolina, coast of South Carolina.

53. Thomas C. Hindman, Arkansas, Kentucky.

54. Adley H. Gladden, Louisiana, Pensacola.

55. John Porter McCown, Tennessee, Kentucky.

56. Llyod Tighlman, Kentucky, Kentucky.

57. Nathan G. Evans, South Carolina, coast of South Carolina.

58. Cadmus M. Wilcox, Tennessee, Army of Potomac.

59. Philip St. George Cocke, Virginia, died in Virginia.

60. R. F. Rhodes, Alabama, Army of Potomac.

61. Richard Taylor, Louisiana, Army of Potomac.

62. Louis T. Wigfall, Texas, Army of Potomac.

63. James H. Trapier, South Carolina, coast of Florida.

64. Samuel G. French, Mississippi, Army of Potomac.

65. William H. Carroll, Tennessee, East Tennessee.

66. Hugh W. Mercer, Georgia, ——.

67. Humphrey Marshall, Kentucky, Kentucky.

68. John C. Breckinridge, Kentucky, Kentucky.

69. Richard Griffin, Mississippi, Army of Potomac.

70. Alexander P. Stewart, Kentucky, Kentucky.

71. William Montgomery Gardner, Georgia, on furlough.

72. Richard B. Garnett, Virginia, Army of Potomac.

73. William Mahone, Virginia, Norfolk.

74. L. O'Brien Branch, North Carolina, coast of North Carolina.

75. Maxey Gregg, South Carolina, coast of South Carolina.

www.ingramcontent.com/pod-product-compliance
Lightning Source LLC
LaVergne TN
LVHW011206110826
845150LV00006B/1341

* 9 7 8 1 4 2 5 5 1 8 2 0 2 *